# THE ART OF PERSUASION

*Στον αδελφούλη μου*

*με αγάπη,*

*Eileen*

# THE ART OF PERSUASION

## How to Influence People and Get What You Want

**JULIET ERICKSON**

HODDER
MOBIUS

First published in Great Britain in 2004 by Hodder & Stoughton
A division of Hodder Headline
This edition published in 2005

The right of Juliet Erickson to be identified as the Author
of the Work has been asserted by her in accordance with the
Copyright, Designs and Patents Act 1988.

A Mobius paperback

10 9 8 7 6 5 4 3 2 1

A CIP catalogue record for this title is available from the British Library

ISBN 0 340 83031 X

Typeset in Sabon by
Phoenix Typesetting, Auldgirth, Dumfriesshire

Printed and bound in Great Britain by
Clays Ltd, St Ives plc

Hodder Headline's policy is to use papers that are natural, renewable and
recyclable products and made from wood grown in sustainable forests. The
logging and manufacturing processes are expected to conform to the
environmental regulations of the country of origin

Hodder & Stoughton
A division of Hodder Headline
338 Euston Road
London NW1 3BH

# ACKNOWLEDGEMENTS

To my clients – for the getting of a certain wisdom and without whom none of this would be possible.

My friends for being generous with their love, encouragement, time and ideas: Betsy Komjathy, Jill Danks, Stewart Pearce, Tim Baines, Peter Lockyer, Henrietta Spink, Philip Carr, Sarah Stacey, Irene Thiele-Muehlhan, Nigel Barnfield, Judy Daly.

Caro Handley, my editor, the queen of her craft.

Peter Rogen, Neil and Marcie Flett and the Rogen International team for over a decade of fun and adventure.

The Hodder team.

Kay McCauley, my agent for her unfailing support, enthusiam and skill.

My family, Ruth, Carol and Lloyd for their unconditional listening.

# ACKNOWLEDGEMENTS

To Stan and Liza

I have always loved the desert. One sits down on a desert sand dune, sees nothing, hears nothing. Yet through the silence something throbs, and gleams.

Antoine de Saint-Exupery

# CONTENTS

# INTRODUCTION

Have you got something you're dreaming of doing? Is there a message you'd like to give the world? Maybe it is a business you'd like to start, a worthy cause that needs your help or an idea you'd like to bring to fruition. Most of us have a dream, something we want or feel compelled to do. What's yours?

In the last fifteen years I have worked with thousands of people, one to one or a few at a time, focusing on one thing: refining the way they communicate so that their key idea or message would get through in the way they wanted and needed it to. So they could win more often. So they could make things happen around them. I have worked in the major commercial centres of the world – Tokyo, Sydney, Singapore, London, New York, Frankfurt, Paris, Toronto, São Paulo, Buenos Aires, San Francisco, Geneva, Zurich and Mexico City, among others.

Some of my clients are responsible for leading and managing vast numbers of people. Some will, over their lifetimes, earn more money than the incomes of many small countries. They have degrees from the best universities around the world and they run some of the world's top corporations and institutions, including those in advertising, law, investment banking, manufacturing, research, not-for-profit agencies and governments.

But no matter how many billions of dollars are at stake, how earth-shatteringly good or important an idea is, or how experienced, famous or clever a person may be, their success largely boils down to one thing: how well they can communicate persuasively with others. Simply put, this ability will determine whether they fail or succeed in what they set out to do.

Being able to communicate in the way we want in order to achieve our goals is our biggest challenge and provides our greatest opportunity for success. Of course, persuasive communication is not the only thing that will grant us all our desires or solve the world's problems. But I can put my hand on my heart and say that in my experience it is a major contributing factor in my clients achieving their personal and professional goals.

So, whatever it is you want to achieve, persuasive communication will be an essential part of it. Communication is central to life – everyone's life. You can't not communicate. Or to put it another way, you have to communicate, like it or not and whether you feel good at it or not. The way you communicate will shape your relationships with others, both publicly and privately, as well as determining what you create for yourself in life. So, why not make sure that you *do* feel good at it?

## MY STORY

My first full-time job was in Sydney, where I lived for a few years after finishing college in the United States. I worked for a couple of dynamic entrepreneurs who were launching a new form of technology on to the Australian market. My job was to persuade people who might benefit from the technology to buy it. I loved it, and the launch was a great success. A couple of years later I moved on to help launch a venture called Australian Geographic – a magazine and a chain of retail stores – which was also very successful.

My next move was to a new young company called Rogen. There I teamed up with another couple of wonderful entrepreneurs. Together we shared a dream about building a global organisation doing what we really loved: persuasive face-to-face communication. We offered potential clients coaching, consulting in high-stakes situations, new-business pitching, leadership training, selling, negotiating and presenting.

At Rogen I found that all the things I had always enjoyed doing came together under one umbrella. By the age of twenty-eight I was a partner there and by the time I left twelve years later we'd grown from a four-person operation in Sydney to an international company employing 150 people worldwide.

I was responsible for developing the United States market in 1992. With little more than the determination to make it work and a telephone, I opened an office in New York. Four years later it employed fifteen people and had a turnover of two million dollars a year. In Los Angeles it was a similar story and after that I went to London to open the first European branch of the company.

Finally, after twelve years of no fixed address, earning more frequent-flyer miles than I can use in a lifetime, lonely boyfriends, seven-day weeks and friends and family wondering whether I existed any more – you get the picture – I decided it was time to change the pace. I sold my stake in Rogen, stayed on in London and carried on doing what I do best: teaching people how to use persuasive communication to enhance their lives. This seemed like the right point to do something I'd wanted to do for a long time – to put all that I'd learned together in a form that anyone could access and use. This book is the result.

It's been born out of my fascination that something so simple and common to all of us – our ability to communicate persuasively – can, at its best, propel us to great heights of achievement and success.

Most of my biggest triumphs have been communication-based. So have my biggest embarrassments and errors of judgement! I've learned as I've gone along and now I'm delighted to be able to pass on the very best of what I've discovered.

## WHAT THIS BOOK WILL DO FOR YOU

This book is about how you can develop and refine your persuasive communication skills and then use them to make the things you want happen. What do I mean by making things happen?

For my friend who organises a charity, improving her persuasive communication skills meant finally winning a long battle with her local authority. She has since attracted the interest of a publisher and is writing a book, which may lead to a film, about her experiences.

For a client who runs one of the largest corporations in the UK and the United States, it meant convincing the shareholders that he was the right person to run the company after a take-over.

To another client, improving his communication skills meant making a lifetime's dream come true by successfully setting up his own business.

For a bright young student, it meant getting a place at her choice of university.

For a determined mum wanting to change things at her child's school for the better, it meant winning a place on the board of governors.

For a senior scientist, it meant convincing the company's board of the merits of his new invention and then being granted the support and funding to put it into production.

And for an artist wanting to find recognition, it meant his first major exhibition and a successful string of sales.

So, what will you gain from reading this book? Here are some realistic expectations:

You will be able to:

- Understand how your personal communication skills affect your life and your ability to make things happen
- Increase your level of awareness and flexibility
- Use your power of persuasive communication to make better choices
- Learn how to successfully plan, prepare and deliver whatever you want to communicate
- Be ready to go for opportunities when they present themselves
- Keep your momentum going once you have achieved your goals and achieve even more

If you're ready to take on the responsibility for making your idea or message real and successful then you'll find the encouragement and practical information you need here. You will learn how you can make an enormous impact on whether you succeed or fail by paying attention to every aspect of your communication. Let me explain how it will work.

The book is broken into three clear and easy-to-follow sections:

First, 'Getting the Basics Right'. This section is about understanding why and how persuasive communication is so critical and then making sure you're absolutely clear about what it is you want to communicate.

By the end of this section, you will be able to clearly define and describe your idea, or message, and identify the key outcomes you want.

The next section will help you put together a 'toolbox' of fundamental communication skills that you can call on when you need them most. The modern world expects us to be communication gymnasts and I want you to be able to do cartwheels!

In the third section I will help you prepare for the most critical make-or-break moments – those times when the stakes are high and you will be called upon to get it right first time. Whether it's a speech, a presentation, a chance to convince someone that your idea will work, a sudden opportunity you want to go for or an interview for the job of your dreams, you'll learn the secrets of how to succeed.

The information in this book comes from a treasure-chest of experience, proven techniques and insights that have worked for people all over the world. It will help you to clarify your own thinking and then communicate your ideas to others in a way that will enable you to make permanent and meaningful changes. As well as learning how to communicate more clearly and persuasively, you will have the opportunity to become a better listener, improve the quality of your relationships and achieve your goals. If you're committed to refining your skills, I promise you will enjoy rewards. Eventually, you will use the skills more naturally, confidently and authentically and, best of all, not have to think about it all too much.

My vision is pretty simple. I want to live in a world where we all wake up in the morning feeling excited and empowered about what we can achieve.

You already hold the key to your success. What I will do is help you to get your message, goal or idea out of your head and turn it into something real. This book is a gift from me, the people I've worked with and those who have guided me in getting it to you. It's my hope that your life will be enriched by what is in it and that as you travel through it you will enjoy the journey.

**PART ONE**

# GETTING THE BASICS RIGHT

# 1

# THROWING OUT THE RULEBOOK

*Communication occurs when anything makes an impression or influences an attitude.*
**PETER ROGEN**

We are all communicating, all the time, whether we know it or not. Everything we do, don't do, say or don't say, gives an impression of us to those we are with, or in touch with. And this opens up a wonderful opportunity. Because every time you communicate you have the chance to do it better, be more effective and create even more successful outcomes.

Communication is more important than it has ever been, in every area of our lives. Poor communication leads to conflict, misunderstanding, disharmony, low self-esteem and failed relationships. Good communication leads to feeling great, being assertive, living in harmony with others and finding success. This applies to our personal lives, our work, our relationships and every other area of our lives. Good, effective communication brings the results we want by giving us the ability to make ourselves clearly understood, to build strong relationships and connections with others and to successfully persuade others to support us.

The corporate world has come to understand this over the last few years. Communication skills have usually been referred to in the business community as 'soft skills'. I've never really known what this means, but for many firms it definitely puts them somewhere pretty low in the corporate pecking order, along with decisions about where to have the next office party and the details of the stationery order.

This attitude changes fast when sales revenues start to drop, clients switch to competitors and the company stands to win or lose millions in a pitch. That's when they realise it's time to call in the communication experts to show them how to turn their businesses around, win back clients and increase revenue. In clever companies communication skills are now high priority, because they understand the role that these skills can play in their success.

If businesses and corporations don't understand the effectiveness of persuasive communication then they lose out. And the same goes for us as individuals. Now, more than ever, good communication skills are vital if we want to pursue our goals and dreams successfully.

This chapter is about the basic principles of persuasive communication. What works, and why it works. These principles are very different to the ones that were used in the past, because right now we're in the middle of a communication evolution. The way we communicate and understand each other has changed enormously in the past thirty years.

Books about communication used to talk about how to 'close the sale', give your 'spiel' or manipulate your listener into doing what you want in order to achieve your objective. But things have changed and the people we need to convince have many more distractions in their lives and far more pressure on their attention spans. As a result they are more demanding and more choosy about what they will pay attention to or include in their lives. The only way to focus their attention and then use this opportunity effectively is to have good communication skills.

Today the principles that make communication effective are based on increased awareness and your ability to be flexible. These principles can and should be adapted according to the situation, the person or people you are with and the message you want to convey. Our individual communication skills also have to be refined and we need better communication tools in order to deal with a range of situations. It's a bit like saying that whereas in the past a hammer might have done the job, now we need a diamond-cutter.

## THE PRINCIPLES OF EFFECTIVE COMMUNICATION

Before we go any further I want to explain what I mean by effective communication. How do we know when what we are doing works or doesn't work? You can measure the effectiveness of your communication very simply by looking at whether or not people have been in some way affected by you. In other words, have you had an impact on them?

What do I mean by an impact? Simply that the other person did something because you asked them to or recommended it, or they made a decision, changed their mind, felt differently or thought about something in a different way because of what you did or said.

Here are my seven principles of effective communication. They're based on my years of experience as a communicator and the many situations in which I have seen communication succeed or fail.

1. Forget rules
2. Build rapport
3. Be yourself
4. Focus on individuals

5. Be definite
6. Actions speak loudest
7. Stay present

With these principles in mind your communication is going to be more powerful and effective.

Why? Because between them they encompass the essence of what you need to shape, and convey your message in a way that is clear and persuasive. Now let me explain each of the principles in a little more detail.

## 1. Forget Rules

This is the first and most important principle of communication in the twenty-first century. What works in one situation won't necessarily work in another. What persuades one person won't persuade the next person. Today we are more discerning, well-informed and busy than ever, so trying to apply 'rules' blanket-fashion to all your communication will leave you wondering why things aren't working.

It's always tempting to learn the 'rules' and follow them because we all tend to use what we're comfortable with over and over again. But this comfort zone can be our biggest threat to communicating effectively. It can create a barrier between us and another person because while the comfort zone 'rules' may work fine in one situation, they won't work in the next or the one after that.

I've spent years undoing the damage inflicted on my clients by academics, popular quick-fix experts, self-help teachings and the desire to look for certainties and rules. So often what the clients thought was going to work didn't and what they thought might fail succeeded brilliantly.

What they needed to learn is that what makes any one of us effective as a communicator depends on the context, the circumstances and the people we are talking to.

When I was visiting my sister in Hawaii recently I met a man who was in the middle of a big fight to save a local beach, near where he lived, from the erosion that was destroying it. He wanted to save the beach for future generations and needed financial support to build a wall to protect it. This meant he had to talk to developers, politicians, conservationists, the town council, the press and people in the street.

His campaign wasn't going well. The problem was that he was applying his own 'rules', believing he was most effective by talking to all these people in exactly the same way and telling the same story in the same way over and over again. It was a powerful story, but doing this simply watered it down so that some people lost interest and others didn't feel it was relevant to them. What he needed to do was to let go of his 'rules' and tailor what he said to address each of the parties' particular interests and level of understanding. That way they would understand the situation more clearly and might see more compelling reasons and, more importantly, exactly what they could do to help to save the beach.

### Awareness and Flexibility

The communication muscles that really work now are awareness and flexibility. These two qualities have replaced all the do's and don'ts that communication 'gurus' got away with in the past. Now the heat is on and there's no getting away with anything; you have to know what really works. With your awareness and flexibility fully developed you can then adapt effectively and appropriately to the situation you are in, tailoring your message to suit the circumstances and the people involved.

### So, what are these special qualities and how do we develop them?

**Awareness** is being awake and alert to what is going on both

inside and around you. The inner and outer aspects of awareness are intricately linked, because when self-awareness
increases, you will automatically become more aware of the
world around you and more sensitive to the needs and reactions of others. To become more self-aware you have to
undertake some self-analysis and ask yourself questions
about why some things work out for you and others don't.
It means concentrating on your strengths while looking hard
at what doesn't work in your life, finding out why and
changing it.

**Flexibility** means that you can respond and adjust appropriately to what you see or know. It means that you have the
ability to adapt according to the situation you are in.
Flexibility follows on from awareness; the greater your
awareness the easier you will find it to be flexible.

Flexibility requires a certain amount of confidence. It
means you can deviate from your plan and still feel in control.
Most important of all, to be flexible you need to cultivate an
open attitude. Approach any situation willing to see what's
going on and to change your approach if you need to.

Using awareness and flexibility you can decide what is
appropriate or inappropriate for a particular context. You
can think on your feet, make decisions as you go along and
change direction when you need to.

All the tools I will give you in part two of the book will
help you to increase your awareness and flexibility. You can
also help to increase them by doing any of the following. I've
seen these work for many others:

- Take up an activity you've never tried before
- Develop a talent you've neglected
- Improve your health
- Ask a friend you trust for feedback about the way you behave
  in different situations

- Meditate
- Get curious and learn about a new subject
- Do yoga

Developing your awareness and flexibility is an on-going process that needs to become an enjoyable and automatic part of your everyday life. In this way your ability to communicate well without relying on 'rules' will become increasingly strong.

## 2. Build Rapport

Choose rapport as your primary objective, rather than 'winning' and you will win more often. In the 'no rules' world of communication, understanding rapport and building it is the way forward. In the past it was believed that you could 'persuade' someone of something without necessarily having rapport. However, the success rate of this approach was pretty low. Today rapport is seen as a vital prerequisite if you want to be successful in persuading other people to accept your message.

What is rapport? The *Oxford English Dictionary* defines it as 'a close relationship where people understand each other and communicate well' and that sums it up nicely. In the end it means removing the differences between us on a very subtle level. Choosing rapport as your objective doesn't mean that you shouldn't care about winning, in fact you have to want to win if you want to be successful in your goal, whatever it is. It's just that winning is very often the result of rapport, rather than the other way around. It's time to put the cart after the horse.

For a long time now Western culture and business have worshipped at the altar of winning. People who are desirable in the world of work are supposed to be dynamic, driven, prepared to stay up all night to prove their commitment, aggressively interested in beating the competition and re-munerated on how much they win. Beating the other person was the goal, no matter what the cost.

The essence of rapport is something quite different. You can sum it up in this way: 'You win, but I don't feel I've lost.' And whatever happens we need the trust and respect that are the foundation of a good relationship, so that whoever wins next time, the relationship is still good. Winning has so many different definitions and takes place in so many different contexts. You will surprise and delight yourself if you let your rapport with others play a large part in defining winning for you.

Not only do many people have winning as their primary objective, but they often lose touch with what it means to win and mistake being busy for winning. Our culture puts a high value on being busy, yet being busy can distract you from what really matters.

If we are trying to make something happen by using persuasive communication, we need to make a subtle shift in the way we approach things and choose consciously to build relationships instead of focusing only on getting what we want or on running from one thing to the next.

A while ago I got to know a woman who is a high-profile politician. She recently had some health problems associated with exhaustion and while she was recuperating I went to visit her for a cup of tea. We began chatting about how her life was changing as a result of her illness and she pulled out a copy of her schedule for the past six months. There were pages and pages of back-to-back meetings, lunches, dinners and speeches. She told me that this schedule represented some of the most unproductive time she has ever spent. At the time she felt a kind of comfort in being 'busy' because it made her feel successful and a 'winner'. But when she reflected on what she had actually achieved, many of the important policy issues had in fact not been dealt with and many of her work priorities were left unfinished. She vowed to focus on the important people she needed to build relationships with and on the issues that really mattered to her. Together we went through her schedule and crossed out the 'busy' meetings – the ones that weren't important for building important relationships or meeting her goals. When we'd finished we had less than half the pages left, leaving her so much more time to focus on winning where it really matters.

With rapport not only will you win more often, you will win on good terms and not at someone else's expense. In the world of work many institutions and businesses are designing 'partnerships' with people they used to compete with. They call it co-opetition. The aim is to build good relationships that result in better deals and higher profits all round. So, what are the factors involved in building rapport? When and why do people feel they have rapport with someone else?

Over the years I have conducted a lot of research into why people are persuaded by one person rather than another and what makes them feel interested or excited by one person's idea and not someone else's.

The answers helped to explain why some of the world's best ideas end up in the rubbish bin. If you can't make an idea meaningful and clear, if you can't build a relationship with the person you're trying to convince, then no matter how good your idea, it's likely to fail.

The results of my research were that people's responses can be divided into three sections:

- 40 per cent of the response was based on whether they felt the idea had merit
- 20 per cent of the response was based on what was

described as 'politics' within a company or organisation
- And finally an astonishing 40 per cent of the response was based on whether they felt a positive personal connection and understanding with the person putting forward the idea

The conclusion of this research was that success in 'selling' an idea depends just as much, if not more, on your rapport with the individuals you are trying to influence as on the idea itself. In other words, rapport is vital for successfully selling an idea or persuading someone of your message. Can you be persuasive without rapport? Well, I can give you a convincing argument about something with which you may fundamentally disagree. You may not know or like me but I may change your view. But I am far more likely to succeed in influencing you if you like me or feel comfortable and at ease with me while you listen to what I have to say.

Your ability to build rapport is the skill that will be responsible for the biggest changes in the way you communicate. When you are building rapport you will encounter opportunities, ideas and energies that are not always visible when winning is your objective. The blinkers come off and you see, hear and feel bigger and better possibilities. Relationships are richer, they last longer and they weather the storms and inevitable mess-ups that happen in life.

The truth is that there's little point in spending time and energy on getting facts and figures right if we don't put energy into understanding the people who will make the decisions and building a positive connection with them.

In chapter 3, 'Building Rapport', I will explain in greater depth how you can learn to build rapport with more people in a greater range of situations, whether you 'click' with them naturally or not.

## 3. Be Yourself

Being yourself means cultivating the ability to feel natural and relaxed in any situation. All too often we get nervous and resort to behaviour that comes across as false and unnatural. We try too hard, smile a little too brightly, act confident and dynamic when we're naturally quiet, or clam up when we'd actually love to talk.

This 'fake' behaviour is usually the result of lack of confidence. We resort to what we feel we 'should' be doing or saying according to rules we've been given, or made up, and lose any sense of what feels right and appropriate for the situation. The trouble is it doesn't work. The chairman of a company I worked for once said, 'You can only fake it for fifteen minutes.' Behaving in a way you think you 'should' will make you appear false and unnatural and this will soon make others feel uncomfortable. When you're faking it the listener can sense something unreal. They don't always know what it is but they can feel it and they won't be attracted to you – or to the ideas you're putting across to them.

When you fake it it's harder to build rapport or to communicate successfully because you can't build a genuine bond with the other person and you can't listen properly. While the occasional trick can be handy in a sticky situation it's always more effective to drop the act and just be yourself.

What does it mean to be yourself? It certainly doesn't mean making no effort, being sloppy in your work, turning up in your pyjamas or putting your feet on the table. Being yourself means being comfortable with yourself, at ease and natural. And that isn't always very easy!

Of course, there are limited exceptions. I once worked with a quirky genius who was always badly dressed with his hair in a mess. He mumbled, rambled and had bad manners. For most people this would be the kiss of death but the clients loved him, first because he was entertaining and second because he really produced results and was such a stellar intellect that he was a novelty.

He got away with it but unless you're a genius, you probably won't, so make sure that 'be yourself' doesn't turn into 'let it all hang out' or 'I'm me and that's that'. When you allow yourself to be open and relaxed you will discover your natural charisma. Most people would like to be considered 'charismatic' and imagine that this is a quality that other people possess. But being charismatic doesn't come from doing anything difficult or complicated or from being glamorous or famous. Communication research over the last thirty years has revealed that what comes across as charisma is really expressiveness. Which means being open and willing to communicate, verbally and non-verbally.

The more natural you feel, the more effective and charismatic you will be. But many people are not willing to risk being 'natural', believing that they will end up damaging their chances of success. They either feel that their 'natural' style is dull or ineffective, or they don't even know what their natural style is like and are reluctant to find out.

Often they resort to well-meaning advisers who teach them to 'do it this way' or 'behave that way'. For example, there is a school of thinking whose advocates coach individuals on how to be better presenters and communicators. I can spot the people who have worked with them because they take on a theatrical air and their voices and movements are unnatural. They look slick, untouchable and arrogant.

Being yourself is about unleashing a power that already belongs to you and lies just beneath the surface: your natural charisma. We all have natural charisma and by bringing it out and polishing it we develop far more effective communication skills. In chapter 10, 'Fixing the Physical', I'll be looking in more detail at how, using simple ways to develop and enhance your natural charisma.

## 4. Focus on Individuals

Effective communication is a two-way exchange between two people – you and one other. Even in a situation where you are addressing more than one person, each person you are trying to influence will decide whether you've affected them or not. So often people think of an audience as an amorphous blob of people. Think of an audience as just one person and your focus and intention will be on talking to individuals. People behave as individuals and are therefore persuaded as individuals even when they are gathered together with a common purpose. Ask each person coming out of a cinema what they thought was important about the film and each one will give you a different answer.

Having put your focus on to the individual you are addressing, the next step in communicating well is to understand this person. And to do this you need to take your attention off yourself and put it on to them. In other words listen and learn whether what you are doing is interesting and relevant to the other person and then find out what you might do to improve it.

So many people make the mistake of trying to improve their communication skills by focusing on themselves. In fact it's far more effective to put the focus on the other person. Real awareness and your ability to cut through to the important issues come from knowing as much as you can about the others you will be addressing.

You'll be surprised how easy it is to say what you want to say when you know something about the person who is listening. The message you want to communicate shapes itself more easily and priorities become clear. When you understand the person you are talking to you can ask more perceptive and well-informed questions. You can demonstrate your own experience and expertise. You can build a stronger rapport and uncover real issues that affect the other person. You'll be calmer, you'll improve your general level of awareness and you'll be able to listen better. Knowing the other person helps you choose what to say and the best way of saying it; and what ideas, facts, words, style and examples will be most convincing to your listener.

James, an Australian entrepreneur, recently launched his first book. It's about his role in building one of Australia's most successful businesses. He told me about his experience of talking to different radio stations during the book launch. One radio station 'audience' was specifically focused on the working man. The interviewer at that station spent almost the whole interview talking about how the business got started twenty years ago from scratch. The financial-business radio station focused mostly on how the company was able to be so profitable despite running risky business in uncertain times. A women's programme focused almost entirely on how his business had more female senior managers than any other business of its type. Same book, same author – different listeners.

In chapter 5, 'Making Your Message Persuasive', I'll be taking a closer look at ways of finding information about and getting to know the person or people you will be communicating with.

## 5. Be definite

If you want to do something, be definite about it. Being definite means having a purpose or a pure, strong intent. When you are definite it brings what you want into the present and allows you to do it and speak about it with genuine conviction and clarity. A friend of mine calls this speaking your mind. I'd add 'and heart'.

You need to be definite about what your idea or message is as well as about the outcome you would like. This doesn't necessarily mean that you know how you'll get to the outcome.

Max, a successful banker, had always loved painting in his spare time. Eventually he decided that he wanted to spend more of his time painting and less time in the office. He was definite about what he wanted but not certain how it would actually happen. So he began by organising small shows at friends' houses and setting up a website of his artwork. He began to sell some of his paintings and was invited to put on a show in a small gallery, followed by another in a larger gallery. After eighteen months Max took the decision to work only three days a week in his office and to spend the other two painting. A year on he was able to give up his office job altogether and paint full-time.

When you are definite about what you want, your commitment to it and the energy you put into it will trigger a response in those around you. If you send out half-hearted energy, you'll get half-hearted energy back. Fully committed energy will get a great response because others will sense your determination and want to support you.

Julia Cameron, in her book *Walking in this World*, says that 'Intention creates direction.' In other words know where you're going and you'll find the way there. Commit to what you want and the 'how' will sort itself out.

### 6. Actions Speak Loudest

Effective communication involves far more than just words. It involves behaviour, appearance, gestures and unspoken empathy as well. People are more influenced by who you are and how you behave than by what you are actually saying. In fact, your words form only a small part of the impression you're making on another person. Your actions, body language and expressions make up the rest.

We often make seemingly outrageous 'snap judgements' about people we don't know or have met only briefly. But they're not so outrageous after all. We base this 'instant' assessment of another person on all kinds of information that we take in at a glance. Their look, dress, style, expression, walk, manner and body language all form part of our impression.

The criteria we use to form impressions of one another are fascinating. Research tells us that only seven per cent of the impression we make comes from the words we use. Well over half of the impression we make comes from the way we act, move, gesture and express ourselves.

In other words, it's not going to be enough simply to know what you want to say and say it. You'll need to pay plenty of attention to the way you dress, walk, gesture and use your voice in order to make sure that these things reinforce what you mean and create a minimum of distraction.

People's impressions matter and they don't have to be right to matter.

I heard recently about a man who had been working hard for months to put together a proposal for a community-funded sports centre. He had worked tirelessly to get corporate support, community representatives and sports enthusiasts behind his idea. He was given time to present his idea at a local-government meeting where the decision-makers would be present. If the idea was successful it meant that he would be running it as a full-time job. It was a great opportunity for him and the community and he needed to come across well and clearly.

On the day things didn't work out very well. The night before the meeting he was sick with food poisoning and up most of the night. In the morning while he and his family were preparing for the day, the plumbing broke and flooded the downstairs rooms. Then the dog ran out of the house and went missing. To cap it all, on the way to the presentation his car overheated and he had to abandon it and take a taxi in order to make it.

He got there just in time, only to be asked to wait for an hour as they were running late. When he was finally asked to present his idea, it was late in the afternoon and he was frazzled and tired. His project was turned down and he was told afterwards that he didn't demonstrate the confidence they felt was necessary to run a project of this size.

Was this fair? Absolutely not, but that's not the point. Often we have a short time in which to make the impressions we need to make. So we must do everything we can to improve our chances.

In chapter 10, I'll be showing you how to become more aware of your non-verbal communication so that your listener will be able to take in what you say in the way that you intend by minimising distractions and the possibility of creating a wrong impression.

## 7. Stay Present

This last principle is hugely important because without it none of the others will work.

The issue of staying present is central to all good and effective communication. What do I mean by staying present? Simply put it means being aware of the moment you are in. So much of the time we are lost in the past or the future. We daydream, remember, plan and look forward but we seldom remain for long right here in the present moment, awake and alert to what is going on around us. Staying present takes practice, but it's well worth the effort. When you stay present you notice so much more of what is going on around you: small changes in energy, looks, little asides and gestures that can give us insight. Things we so often miss but which can affect the mood and the tone of whatever is going on. Staying present is empowering, energising and exciting. When you can stay present then the communication tools I will give you will immediately become more effective, more natural and easier to use.

To encourage yourself to stay present, begin noticing the reality and the detail of what is going on around you. Pay attention to the present. A good way to start is by noticing your own behaviour, reactions, thoughts, fears and distractions. Gently push aside thoughts of past and future and focus on the moment you are in. Then watch what happens!

## YOUR MESSAGE

So, besides applying the principles I've outlined above, what else do you need to do to get your communication right and make things happen in the way that you want?

The most important thing is to create a clear idea of exactly what you want and why you want it. This may sound pretty obvious but you'd be amazed how many people just 'do things', or not, for the sake of doing them, or not, and never really think about whether these things are actually what they want.

They're doing what they've been told to do, or seen others do, or find easiest. But none of those is a good enough reason for doing something and none of them is likely to lead to great success. You need to work out what you really want and then follow it with passion and determination.

Once you know exactly what you want you can start to tell others about it. A big part of successful persuasion is letting people know that you want it and learning to articulate, very simply, what your project, idea or goal is all about, without waffling, apologising or beating about the bush.

It's not always easy to sum up an idea, especially if it's one that has been close to your heart for a long time. It isn't easy to answer questions about it when you're put on the spot by someone at a function or a party. It takes thought and practice to have the information ready and to be able to produce it easily to anyone, at any time.

But getting absolutely clear about what you want and then learning to tell others about it, briefly and clearly, is an essential step towards achieving it. Once you've done this you'll be ready to press the 'go' button and to put all your energy into the one thing that will make a real difference: the way you communicate.

That's why, before we move on to the toolbox of skills you're going to need, the next chapter will help you look in detail at your message, whether it's right for you and just how badly you want to make it happen.

# 2

# YOU CAN'T CROSS
# HALF A BRIDGE

*Press on; nothing in the world can take the place of
perseverance. Talent will not; nothing is more
common than unsuccessful men with talent. Genius
will not; unrewarded genius is almost a proverb.
Education will not; the world is full of educated
derelicts. Persistence and determination are
omnipotent. Press on*

**CALVIN COOLIDGE**

One of the biggest challenges I come across as a communication coach is the potential gap between a person's stated
objective or idea and whether or not they are ready or willing
to make it happen.

In many cases a person will know what they want, they'll
have identified their goal or aim yet there will be a sense of
doubt around it. This doubt usually boils down to one of two
causes. Either they don't actually want the goal, they simply
feel they ought to want it. Or they truly want it but doubt
their ability to achieve it.

When this gap appears, between the stated goal and the
will to make it happen, then the whole project will inevitably

run into problems. It's like trying to cross half a bridge. It won't get you anywhere and the idea or goal will lack clarity, force and believability. It will be tough going to 'make something of it'; in these circumstances I can end up battling with the client's cynicism, short temper, heel-dragging, lack of preparation and lack of understanding about what it is going to take to succeed.

When this happens the chances of success are slim.

That's why, before we go any further, I want to focus on helping you to get your intention right. When you have intention then you have more than just your goal and the will to persevere. Intention is the older, smarter sister of perseverance; it puts a pointed edge on perseverance by giving it purpose.

Having intention is the difference between wanting to do something and wanting to do something enough that you will keep going and not be deterred by the setbacks that arrive in your path. This is not about being bloody-minded but knowing obstacles are there to be walked around rather than pushed aside!

Intention has a special quality that makes it your most powerful tool in reaching your goal. It gives you the meaning and momentum to cross the other half of the bridge. When you have clear intention it sets you apart from others and gives you the kind of positive energy that people around you can see and feel. They are influenced and excited by it and things start to happen.

This chapter is divided into two sections. The first looks at your intention levels and the blocks you may unwittingly be putting in the path of your intention. By clearing those blocks you can allow your intention levels to rocket and your achievement level to soar.

After that I'll show you how to focus your intention by creating your Key Message. This is a clear and simple summary of what your project, idea or goal is all about. Your Key Message will allow you to get your idea across to the people you want to persuade, at any time in any place without stumbling, fumbling or bumbling.

## GETTING THE GOAL RIGHT

Have you identified your goal, your dream or the idea or project you want to pursue? Do you know what it is you want to achieve?

Take a little time to be sure that what you're saying you want is really what you want. Because if it isn't, if you don't believe in what you're setting out to do, then it won't work.

Why would anyone set out to do something they don't believe in? There are lots of reasons. It may be that your job requires that you pursue this goal. Perhaps you're up for a promotion, required to do more public speaking or have a productivity goal to achieve.

Or it may be that your family has urged you to reach for this goal. I once met a beautiful girl who had always been told by well-meaning family and friends that she should be a model. So, without thinking too much about it, she became a model. And hated it. It took her several years to jump off that particular bandwagon, work out what she wanted for herself and retrain as a counsellor helping underprivileged children.

Plenty of people become doctors because their parents are doctors, or teachers because their parents are teachers. Others decide to do the opposite of whatever their parents are doing, but that's not a great idea if you're doing it for the sake of it and not because it's what you want.

When I come across clients who don't really believe in the goal they've asked me to help them achieve, then I suggest they review it. Perhaps the goal needs adjusting, rethinking or throwing out. Perhaps it's simply masking the real goal.

Alan, a high-powered equity fund manager, asked me to help him with his presentation skills. It soon became clear, though, that his heart wasn't in it and when I asked him to rethink what he wanted he shyly told me that he actually longed to get out of finance and set up his own cabinet-making business. Once we focused on that instead he raced towards his goal, because his intention was clear and backed by the energy of his excitement.

Sometimes the goal isn't clear because the person's passion and persistence become the driving force. That is, the means becomes more important than the end. When this happens you find bucket loads of energy being thrown in the wrong direction. Result? Frustration all round.

A client of mine told me of a time when he was so determined to get a particular job that when they told him 'no thanks' he became like a bull with a red rag. He pursued it and pursued it, only to find that when he did eventually get the job his triumph was short-lived because he didn't much like it. The job wasn't the right one for him but he'd put all his effort into getting it and almost none into finding out whether it really suited him. He learned a wonderful lesson about his desire to win.

The last thing I want is to encourage you to do something you don't really believe in. So take a few minutes to think about your stated goal and ask yourself whether this is truly what you want, what matters to you and what you believe in. Ask yourself the following three questions:

1. Can you imagine pursuing this goal no matter what hiccups and failures you meet along the way?
2. Does thinking about your goal give you a charge of excitement and energy?
3. Is this goal about more than just making money?

If the answer to these questions is 'no' then put this particular goal to one side for a moment and look at what else you want to achieve. The goal that really matters to you, that makes your senses buzz and brings a smile to your face, will be there.

That's the one to go for. And once you've found your goal you can begin to develop and refine the communication skills that will enable you to make it happen.

## YOUR INTENTION CHECK

Now that you are sure of what it is you want to do or achieve, let's move on to the kinds of blocks you might be putting in your own path.

Why would any of us block ourselves? There's only one answer to that: fear. There are all kinds of fears that surface when you set out to achieve a goal that defines and stretches you. There's fear of failure, fear of success, fear of change, fear of not being good enough and fear of standing up to be counted. And that's just for starters.

Getting your intention clear is about facing your fears full in the face and finding the courage to carry on anyway.

Most of our fears are based on what we've come to believe we can and can't do, or can and can't have in life. We mask these fears by allowing distractions to keep us from achieving our goals.

How often have you said, 'I'd love to do it, but . . .' or 'I just haven't the time/money, energy right now . . . ' or 'I'm going to do it after I've paid the mortgage off/brought the kids up/given up the day job.' There are a million versions of these 'not right now' excuses. They're pretty handy, because if you're too busy to follow your dream then you needn't face the fact that actually you might just be too scared to follow it.

I've identified three bad habits that people commonly fall into when they're putting off doing what they really want to do. This is true whether what you want to do is change careers, start a business, help a charity, get in shape or simply have a straight, honest talk with your boss/partner/mother.

I call these bad habits intention-killers because they're about what you think you can and can't achieve and they stand in the way of you going for what you want. Identify these bad habits and you can choose to bypass them and get your intention crystal-clear and ready to go.

These bad habits are:

1. It's just not my thing
2. I'm waiting for the right moment
3. I know I'm right

## Bad Habit One: It's Just Not My Thing

The 'It's just not me' syndrome stems from the values, beliefs and experiences that all add up to your own personal definition of who you are and what you can achieve or have in life.

This syndrome is rooted deep in your past and all kinds of influences have helped to create and shape it, including family, friends, school, church and life experiences. By the time you're an adult it's automatic, you don't think about it much, but you live your life by the rules it imposes.

You know that 'It's just not me' is going on when you say, or hear, things like:

- I'm not really good at selling myself
- I hate making calls to people I don't know
- They probably wouldn't want to see me if I tried to set up a meeting
- Approaching others is not really my style
- I just wouldn't know where to start

- It gives me the creeps to ask for money
- People are too busy to listen to me
- They'll give me a hard time
- I couldn't ask for that
- I don't have enough experience

When you're operating from the 'It's just not me' part of your-self then you're going through life with blinkers on, narrowing your view of your own potential. This is a major communication default and when it kicks in it can block you from moving forward at any point along the way to your goal.

Of course, we all have values and beliefs that help and support us. Those are great. But the ones that hold us back and keep us scared are the ones we want to root out and change.

There are two types of values that influence us, con-sciously or unconsciously, to live our lives in the way that we do and to make the choices we make.

The first type are based on past experiences and the second type are based on 'rules' which you choose to live by in your life now. These two types of values, past-experience values and rules values, are not mutually exclusive.

Values created by your past experience have developed from a combination of factors: the influence of parents, grandparents and family, the influence of a teacher or our first boss when we started work and the sum total of all the good and bad experiences we've had – the rip-offs, the embarrass-ments, the frustrations, the enjoyments and the achievements.

Some of these we talk about, while others may be so deep that we never talk about them. These values are often linked to very personal and emotional events and experiences. They are like an ever-present inner agenda we only half acknowl-edge is there.

Sandra is a talented scriptwriter who has a dream of getting her work published for use in children's theatre. She believes that she's not really very 'good at selling herself', so she never pursues talking to the right people about what she wants. She sees people who sell themselves as self-centred and pushy and this is blocking her. The belief that there are 'creative' people who don't sell and 'pushy' people who do goes back to her childhood.

The rules values are the ones imposed on us by current circumstances, including our work environment, relationships, financial constraints and lifestyle choices. There are also times when these two sets of values can come into conflict with one another and when this happens a past-experience value will often override a rules value. For instance, if your past-experience value is that you deserve whatever you want then you may find a way to buy a luxury even if your rules value is that you can only spend on essentials.

### Choosing Your Values
The first part of this exercise will help you to identify the values and the beliefs based on these values that may be holding you back. In the second part you can learn to choose new, more supportive, values and beliefs.

### Step One: Identifying Your Values
Take a pen and paper and writes down ten values you have, based on your past experience. Choose five that support you and five that block you.

Here are some examples from my clients of values created by past experiences:

### Values that support

- If you put in effort you'll get results
- Change can be a good thing

- I can achieve whatever I set out to do
- I attract good luck
- I'm a fast learner

### Values that block

- You get what you pay for
- Selling is sleazy
- I don't trust anyone who doesn't look me in the eye
- Most things don't work out
- I don't deserve success

Here are some examples of rules values:

### Values that support

- I'm working towards the lifestyle I want
- I use money with care
- Flexible working is a good idea
- Being your own boss is fun
- Holidays are important

### Values that block

- My budget is very tight
- There's never enough time to get to what I want to do
- Work is boring
- Life is full of demands
- There are no nice bosses

By writing down these influencing values you become more aware of the agendas that can support you or block you. The 'It's just not me' that blocks you is a habit that has its basis in these values and that can undermine anything you set out to do. Take the ones that don't support you and challenge them in the following way:

## Step Two: Changing Your Beliefs

If you refuse to go along with undermining beliefs, or to let them be important then they won't be. Choose instead the beliefs you'd like to have, the ones that support and encourage you and that open up possibilities and opportunities. Spend a little time writing out three to five new beliefs you would like to have from now on.

### Exercise One: The Dynamind Exercise

There's a simple exercise I came across some time ago which is great for working on mental and emotional – as well as physical – problems. I've used it myself and recommended it to many clients and it seems to work for everyone. The technique doesn't heal or change anything, but it prepares the body and mind for healing and change to happen more easily.

1. Choose a physical, mental or emotional problem to work on.
2. Bring both hands together with your fingertips touching.
3. Make the following statement, aloud or silently; 'I have a problem that I can change; I want the problem to go away.'
4. With two or three fingers tap these points seven times each: the centre of your chest, the outer area between the thumb and index finger of both hands, the bone at the base of your neck.
5. Inhale with your attention focused on the top of your head then exhale with your attention on your toes.

Repeat the above steps for continued benefit.

For more details visit www. alohainternational. org

### Exercise Two: Talk the Talk

Scientists have proven that the more times you repeat something (out loud if possible, but to yourself is fine, too) the more firmly it is lodged in your memory. Repeat it enough times and it becomes part of your way of thinking. So every time you find yourself thinking about a belief that doesn't support you, stop yourself immediately and replace it with one of your new beliefs. Then concentrate on this thought and repeat it to yourself as many times as you can. Find ways to integrate it into your life and make it real.

Sue makes crafts that she sells at the local markets and to small retailers. They are beautiful little unique pieces of art that are well received and treasured by those who buy them. But Sue had a real problem when it came to charging for her work. She began by charging only what it cost for the materials to make her pieces. When I asked her why she charged so little she said, 'I couldn't charge more for them. People will think I am ripping them off.'

I pointed out that she was placing no value on the time, effort or creativity she put in to her artwork. Why was this?

Sue thought back and remembered that at school her favourite teacher thought art was a waste of time and encouraged her in academic subjects. This experience had obviously gone very deep and now that she was an artist Sue felt unable to value her work.

Once she understood this connection Sue decided she would begin to value her artistic talents. She began to charge a fair price for her work and to feel good about this.

I worked recently with a senior managing director of an investment bank. Fred had worked in the industry for more than thirty years and was well respected by his peers and colleagues. He had recently been told that his communication style was unclear, he appeared unapproachable and came across as monotonous, dispassionate and lacking energy. In other words, people were getting bored and distracted as they listened to him. As we discussed this I noticed that he had some interesting views about his situation. He believed that 'creating emphasis with certain words or gestures as one spoke was "showy" and could come across as acting.' He believed that when his listeners really understood the subject, 'it was not necessary' to be expressive and that to be 'understated' carried a weightier message.

Fred's values about public speaking were based on the rules values his first boss had taught him and were clearly undermining his performance. Once he saw this he was able to learn how to present in a far more interesting way. To his surprise, when he spoke with more expression and colour and adpated himself more to his listeners, he found that he enjoyed the whole experience more himself and others, too, understood and enjoyed it.

## Bad Habit Two: I'm Waiting for the Right Moment

The way you communicate is a result of the way you think and feel about yourself and the world around you. What is going on inside you is what is going on outside you.

This is particularly true of the second bad habit, waiting for the right moment. This can be the oldest excuse in the book for not doing anything about what you want.

Most of us mistake waiting for trusting. We say, 'I know the right moment will come.' We wait for the right time, the right relationship, the right move, the right opportunity. Waiting looks for answers in the past and creates obstacles; it makes you tired and frustrated because nothing ever happens. When you're in a state of waiting the world waits around you. To make things happen you need to take action. Waiting is like sitting in a car stuck on one spot with the wheels spinning. You think something is happening, but it isn't.

It's an approach that will have a bearing on every encounter you have. It will affect the way you listen and respond and the way others respond to you. Waiting, procrastinating, putting off and inertia of any kind are all a result of fear. We keep ourselves stuck and fail to move forward and this conveys itself to everyone around us. Many of us fear having the thing we want most. What would we do with success? What would we dream about then? What if there were no obstacles to complain about? What if we really deserved to have everything go right?

Behind waiting lies self-doubt. Can you really make this happen? Are you really up to it? Better, surely, to wait for a sign or a moment that seems right. Self-doubt can be paralysing.

What's the solution? I find that the most effective way to combat self-doubt and the inertia it can produce is to behave your way out of it. Change your behaviour by doing something new and your feelings will follow. In other words, don't wait to feel better before you act differently; act differently and you'll be surprised by how quickly you feel better.

Sarah was being promoted to run a division of the publishing company she worked for. She had started in this company as a personal assistant and over the years had become very successful. Now, she was going to be reporting to the board, to shareholders and at company-wide meetings on a regular basis. As the start date for her new position approached, Sarah was getting very nervous and uncomfortable about the promotion and many of the things she was doing simply weren't working out. She couldn't understand why lately she was getting resistance instead of support from her peers and some of her initiatives weren't getting the follow-through she needed. Increasingly worried by the way things were going, she was slowing down and failing to meet deadlines.

After spending some time with her and watching her in action, I asked her if she felt she deserved this promotion.

Sarah broke down in tears and said that she was self-conscious about having started as a secretary and felt that no one really believed she could do the job. Despite being hugely capable she felt like an impostor.

This self-doubt was clear to see in her physical behaviour. She was blushing. Her voice was tight and higher than it normally was and she looked tense and uncomfortable. In every encounter she was sending a message about her negative self-belief and people were responding.

Rather than analyse her long-standing and probably deep-seated lack of self-worth, I encouraged her to change her physical behaviour so that it more closely matched her goals.

By making her more aware of what she was doing she was able to work on stopping it. She began to stand, walk, act and speak with a confidence she didn't at first feel. But by the time she took up her new position bit by bit her confidence levels had soared and she was more than ready.

John was the CEO of a major venture capital company. He was known as one of the best in the business at raising money and managing his client relationships. He had a reputation for his polished performances in the boardroom and in meetings. He called me because he had recently been feeling nervous and uneasy in the lead-up to meetings and in the meetings themselves and it was affecting the quality of his communication. He couldn't figure out why.

After discussing it for a while, he told me that recently there had been a lot of emotional upheaval and the death of one of his parents. He knew this had affected him deeply and had clearly shaken his confidence and focus. We needed to get him 'back on his feet' by fixing the physical things, the actions that he needed to take in order to rebuild his confidence.

This meant better preparation and more involvement in his face-to-face meetings, stronger clearer structures for his messages, a greater awareness of his physical movement, more insight about the clients before he met them and organised rehearsals. With this kind of detailed effort he now felt he had more control over the outcomes of the meetings and better understanding of the individual relationships. He has started to relax and get excited again about new business and public speaking and was able to put aside his fears and doubts and get back on track.

If you are stuck in self-doubt or playing the waiting game you must set aside any excuses for not doing what you want and focus on reasons to do it. This means wiping negativity and self-imposed obstacles off your radar screen and trusting yourself more. Trust that you will do what you need to do when you need to do it.

I don't want you to spend your precious time pondering over why you can't do something. I ask you to be brave. Get on with it. All of us from the most accomplished to the eager beginner have to wrestle with fears and doubts. Don't let the blocks or fears keep you from beginning your quest – don't expect to make them disappear or to feel fearless before you can move forward. Just build a different relationship with the fear.

To make a real change you need to let go of the things that don't serve you: a bit like packing only what you need instead of cartloads of stuff you think you might need. It may take a bit of planning and effort but you'll be glad you did it.

*Exercise: Letting Go of Self-Doubt*

Take one action every day to move yourself towards your goal. It could be anything from writing a letter or making a call to drawing up a master plan or a piece of creative work.

Do the thing you're most afraid of first. Find the thing you're putting off – the scary call, request or visit you need to make – and then do it, straight away. Cultivate self-belief by telling yourself 'I can do this' as often as you can. Practise trusting yourself: go ahead with a personal physical challenge you have previously avoided because you didn't think you could do it. This might be anything from running a marathon to taking up a new hobby. Or maybe it means being alone more often, sitting in silence or putting yourself in new situations.

Instead of waiting for things to happen and calling it trusting, start trusting yourself to make them happen. Trust is like a magnet for the things you want for yourselves and others. When you trust yourself you will listen to others and yourself more fully, you will learn and understand more and your desires will start to become real.

### Bad Habit Three: I Know I'm Right

Bull-headed perseverance can lead you down a slippery slope. I see this as a bad habit because it often happens that people get so enthusiastic about something that they lose sight of the goal and get caught up in the process. By being determined to be right they actually misplace their purpose and defuse their intention. They forget to step back and take a breath and try a little objectivity. They become too focused on winning at all costs and charging ahead and they forget to check whether what they are catapulting themselves towards is really the right thing for them. They may even lose sight of what they really want because of the thrill of victory.

You must be sure that your passion alone is not the main driving force. By all means be passionate about your goal, but remember that achieving the goal that's right for you is what matters, not just careering blindly forward. Always stop to check that what you are heading towards is still what you really want. And make sure the route you use to get there is one that works. This may involve checking it with others who will question what you are doing or the way you are doing it. If you're willing to be questioned then your approach is healthy. Passion can diminish your ability to hear the truth. It can and will blind you. So, be willing to temper your passion with openness and good judgement.

Lulu, a management consultant, was raising money for her Boston marathon sponsorship. She was deeply committed to a young person suffering from multiple sclerosis and decided that in order to make her 'voice' heard among the thousands of other people soliciting for the charitable dollar, she would try to do something really clever. So, she made a special professional offer to a potential donor company for some private individual consulting. The offer was actually very generous and she wrote a heartfelt letter. Before she sent it, she called a few of her friends to test the letter. All her friends liked it with only a few modifications. Everything seemed fine – until she sent it to the target company she hoped would take up the offer and sponsor her. They gave her good feedback about why it wouldn't work technically and gently declined her offer. No one else took up her offer either and Lulu ended up collecting only half the amount she had hoped for.

Only afterwards did she realise that she had only run her letter past people she knew would like it. She actually didn't want to hear that it could fail. She didn't think about why people wouldn't want it or couldn't do it. She wished she had asked someone who might have pointed out the flaws in the idea.

Being determined that you are right can lead to things going wrong. Be open to the opinions of people who may disagree with you. A good idea can be questioned and still stand strong. Modifications can often make a good plan great.

So, it's important not only to determine why your idea is special and different and to ask whom the idea will benefit, but to consider the unthinkable: why might someone *not* support it?

*Exercise: Testing Your Idea*

Ask a friend or colleague what they think someone else might see wrong with the idea.

Try the idea out on a stranger – perhaps a friend of a friend – and ask for an honest opinion.

Come up with three possible flaws in your idea which might put people off it and see whether you can improve on it. Take a deep breath for this one and be honest.

If you pick your friends' brains be sure to include the ones who might point out the flaws in your idea and be willing to listen. That way you'll often get a more candid answer and a new slant on the whole thing and a chance to think honestly and carefully about why something won't work, as well as why it will.


## FIRING UP YOUR INTENTION

Now that you've spotted and shifted any bad habits that might be getting in the way of your intention you can concentrate on firing up your intention to its fullest, most effective and exciting level. I want you to feel that you simply have to get going. That bringing your idea or project to fruition feels absolutely right. Right enough to begin now. I want you to be calm enough to stay focused and yet excited enough to plough through obstacles.

The level of intention you will need to follow something through, particularly when you have generated it can be formidable. But if it is the right thing for you it is amazing how effortless it can feel. Obstacles and problems fall away when you have the right goal, high intention levels and great communication skills. It's an unbeatable package.

To keep your intention levels high you've got to be prepared. You need to enjoy the idea of being in more control of your life and responsible for your own success. And you need to be ready to support yourself emotionally, spiritually and financially as you work towards your goal.

To check your intention levels, ask yourself the following questions. Are you willing to

- Go against conventional wisdom?
- Make lifestyle changes?
- Make personal sacrifices?
- Do homework and learn from others?
- Commit to a plan with no guarantees of success?
- Fail in order ultimately to succeed?
- Trust yourself more?
- Keep going until you accomplish your goals?
- And you have the support of your friends and people on whom you rely?

If you can answer yes to these questions then your intention levels are fantastic and you're ready to go. If you answer no to more than two then you need to re-examine your goal to see whether it's the right one for you.

## When it's Working . . .

Here's a little encouragement. I've put together a list of the things I've noticed about people who have a great level of intention. This is what will be happening to you when it's working for you.

- The idea and how to do it become simple
- You will feel consistently enthusiastic about it (there's a dose of fear now and then, but enjoy it!)
- The things you need and want will start to appear

- You will know what you need to do to engage with others at the level of the heart as well as the mind
- People will seek you out for your advice
- You won't be wedded to one fixed outcome
- You'll laugh a lot more
- Other people will be interested in what you are doing and will be excited enough to tell others about it
- Time will 'fly' while you are thinking/talking/doing it
- You won't have to work 'too hard' on it
- You'll feel good

High intention feels great. It's motivating and energising. So get your intention levels up and keep them going with regular doses of self-encouragement, praise and support.

## YOUR KEY MESSAGE

Your Key Message will get your idea out of your head and help you switch on the 'go' button. It needs to be clear, relevant and simple enough that you can easily and confidently tell others about it.

I love Key Messages because they're the short cut to understanding. They're the verbal equivalent of a rodeo – roping and tying your ideas. Once you get your Key Message right you can use it to build the stories you tell about your project and you can tailor it to suit whatever listener you might be with.

Your Key Message is your answer when someone asks, 'So, what is your idea?' or 'What do you want from me?' Keep it as conversational, brief and straightforward as possible.

Your Key Message helps you to help the listener. It should leave the other person clear about what your project or idea is and wanting to know more. Putting together a Key

Message is vital, otherwise it's so easy to get tongue-tied, repeat yourself or go on for far too long and bore the other person to death. Preparing Key Messages focuses you and makes things less overwhelming. It puts your ideas into bite-size chunks that can be far more easily digested.

There are two steps involved in putting together a Key Message. The first is to get the wording right, so that you feel it sums up what you want to say. The second is to practise it until you sound fluent and relaxed. Get a friend to help out by listening and letting you know when it's not clear or natural enough.

Only recently I was working with a couple of young entrepreneurs who were preparing for an important pitch to a venture-capital company. They're bright people and they offer a brilliant service, but I sat for an hour, got confused and had no idea what on earth they were talking about.

The problem was that they were using their language and there was no way for me to understand what the value was to me, the client. They needed to literally translate what they were saying into simple, clear terms that anyone could understand and find useful.

When you construct your Key Message, put yourself in the shoes of the person who is going to hear it. You also need to think in terms of how the listener might describe you to someone else.

Keep it as basic and simple as you can. When you're finished, ask yourself if it says what you really mean. Does it sound like you? Can you say it without cringing? If not, keep working. It's worth it.

### Putting together your Key Message

Let's get going. In order to get to your Key Messages you need first to know your objective and your intended outcomes.

What are an objective and an outcome?

Take sailing as an example: an objective is your desire to get to Port A. That's pretty clear.

The outcomes are the things you want to think, feel or do, or want others to think, feel or do as a result of your objective. In this case the outcomes may include arriving safely, doing some exploring, enjoying the company of the others on board and practising the navigation skills you learned in your sailing class. Don't be wedded to absolutely fixed outcomes because life, like a sailing trip, doesn't always give you exactly what you plan! Be prepared to roll with it. People who stick too firmly to specific outcomes set themselves up to be unhappy and frustrated. Know the objective, identify the desired outcomes, be flexible and you are more likely to influence what happens – and enjoy it along the way.

OK. What's your objective? This is the one-sentence description of what you would like to happen. An objective is simple, direct and must be free from negative language.

For example: I would like to have an exhibition at my house featuring Tim's art. Or: I would like to start a drop-in centre for teenagers in our neighbourhood.

Then, state your desired outcomes. Remember the outcomes are what you want you or other people to think, feel or do as a result of the objective.

For example: My key outcome for the art exhibition is to introduce many more people to Tim's work and appreciate his talent (*think*). I would also like them to buy what they like (*do*) and to have fun so they tell others (*feel*).

My outcomes for the drop-in centre are to get teenagers to come along (*do*) and enjoy themselves (*feel*) and to find support from others who think the centre is a valuable asset to the neighbourhood (*think*).

Now you are ready for the Key Message itself. Key Messages are made up of four parts:

1. What you want.
2. Why you want it.
3. Who says it's so: this includes information indicating whether something is true or valid and might include research, statistics etc.
4. Relevance: What does it mean to me, the listener? A friend calls this the 'ram-home'.

Back to my art exhibition. This is the Key Message I would give to someone I really wanted to come to the exhibition. This is a busy person who gets asked to a lot of functions. But, having done my homework, I also know that they occasionally support new artists and that they are renovating their house.

'I'm having an art exhibition at my house on 22 May and I'd like you to come. (*what*)

'Tim is an experienced and talented but unknown artist and I thought it would be nice to get some like-minded people together, have a glass of champagne and look at his work. (*why*)

'He has just been accepted as a member of the UK Artists Association and has done a lot of private commission work for people. We've had about thirty acceptances so far and some of them are from gallery owners around town. You can have a look at his website. There are some critical reviews there. (*who*)

'I thought it would be useful and fun for you to meet Tim, given your support of new artists. You may want to talk about what he might be able to do for you after your renovations.' (*relevance*)

How could they say no?

To the teen drop-in centre. You are speaking to friends at a party and they ask about your idea. These friends don't have teenage children but they do live in the community and could support in many other ways.

'I'd like to set up a drop-in centre for teenagers in our neighbourhood. You may have heard about them – they're centres where kids can go and meet each other and have fun after school. (*what*)

'Our neighbourhood has a high percentage of teenage children now and will have even more in the next few years. There is no organised safe and interesting place for them to meet. (*why*)

'Towns like ours that have already set up centres say they are used by over 90 per cent of the local kids. The police also report a significant decrease in teen-related incidents and the kids have also voted them their "favourite place". (*who*)

'It's not just parents who have benefited. Local business people and others donate their time and act as mentors, teachers and friends.' (*relevance*)

When you put together your own Key Message it helps to practise your answers with a partner or friend until you're comfortable rolling them clearly and concisely off your tongue, tailored to a range of situations. I've had my clients practising these messages while walking down hallways, in lifts, on the bus and in the bath.

One client told me how he was lucky to have practised his Key Message so well. Someone he had been trying to get hold of for months to talk about an employment opportunity had turned up at a neighbourhood barbecue. When my client was introduced to him his newborn baby had just thrown up on his jacket and he was busy wiping it off. But he was ready with his Key Message: clarity under pressure!

Your Key Message will prove fantastically helpful to you in two ways. First of all it's helped you to clarify your idea. And second it gives you a clear and strong answer for the many times along the way when you'll be asked about your idea – particularly those times when you're talking to someone who can influence, help or support you.

Now, with your Key Message finely tuned and on hand for any occasion you're ready for the next step. It's time to open the toolbox and get to know the indispensable, easy-to-use and fun communication tools that I have ready for you.

# PART TWO

# THE TOOLBOX

# 3

# BUILDING RAPPORT

*People have one thing in common: they are all different*
**ROBERT ZEND**

Now it's time to start putting together the tools you're going to use to hone and refine your communication skills. The next section of the book will focus on these tools and the easiest and most effective ways to use them. I want you to think of this section of the book as a toolbox from which you can choose the items you need for the task in hand. They're all valuable, but some will be more useful for certain situations, others for different ones. They're not in any particular order, so use them as you need them.

There's one, though, that stands out from the rest because it's so vital and uniquely powerful. Of all the tools I'll give you, the ability to build rapport is the most important. This is the one you'll always need, whatever the occasion or whoever you're dealing with. Without it, no matter what else you have done, learned or prepared, you are far less likely to succeed.

Rapport is far more than liking or being liked. It adds trust to liking and through this gives the connection between two people an extra dimension. Rapport comes from the fifteenth-century French word *rapporter*, meaning the sound of gunfire as it echoes back to you. And that's what it's about, giving out and getting back in equal balance.

But surely, I hear you say, rapport either happens or it doesn't. You either get on with someone or you don't. Lucky if you do, too bad if you don't. Especially if your hopes, dreams and aspirations are riding on the relationship. Not much you can do about it.

That's where you're wrong. I've had hundreds of clients tell me that rapport is 'natural' and can't be cultivated. And when I tell them that of course it can, they are usually sceptical. But every one of them has, after a few sessions learning the fundamentals of rapport-building, realised that it's not only possible to build rapport, it's fun and it can be easier than you think.

Of course, when it happens naturally, that's great. There's a beautiful mystery about the chemistry between people when it works instantly and powerfully. But in most situations, especially those where we need something from someone else, rapport doesn't come about so smoothly and easily. We need to put in a little effort to build it. And when we do, wonderful things can happen. The ability to build rapport will give you a powerful edge, a better chance of achieving your goals and the kind of confidence that will take you wherever you want to go.

Why build rapport? Why not! You're going to have a relationship of some sort with anyone you're communicating with. So, why not make it a good, productive one that you'll both enjoy? If you do you'll gain insight and create a relationship strong enough to weather storms and mishaps when they inevitably happen. Choosing to build rapport means choosing to create the best possible outcome for any meeting or situation you're in. And your ability to build rapport will give you a much better chance when you're faced with someone you don't know who has to make a decision about you.

Some people have asked me whether building rapport is actually just about manipulation. Well, the truth is that we often manipulate each other. It's not a dirty word, simply what happens between people naturally. And if building rapport is a kind of manipulation then it's the best possible kind because it's about creating a comfortable environment in which real communication can take place – and everyone wins.

Building rapport is simply doing what comes naturally, but doing it with awareness. The principles of rapport-building which I will outline in this chapter are based on what happens between two people when there is a natural connection and good communication.

## GETTING IT WRONG

There has been a lot of misunderstanding for a long time, particularly in the business world, about what it takes to build rapport with clients. All businesses want to create an environment in which they and their clients can benefit one another, but they've often gone about it in all the wrong ways, throwing out money, energy and effort and getting nowhere.

Many companies have set about building good relation-ships with their clients by giving their salespeople a directive to 'get in front of clients and see them as often as possible'. And off they go, hitting the phones and clocking up the hours in an effort to get face to face with clients. The problem is that no one worked out what was supposed to happen once they got the meetings. And mostly they ended up being aimless get-togethers. These are known as fly-bys or bird-calls because like a bird flying overhead they sail past and all that's left behind is the bird-mess on the windscreen.

This is why for every busy salesman like this there are five clients trying hard not to see him.

At a more 'sophisticated' level, companies are spending millions of pounds or dollars of shareholders' money on sporting events, trips, gifts and special dinners to woo their clients. But while these lavish events are great entertainment they don't work on their own.

I've seen professionals network like this for months, getting to know someone on a social level, and get nowhere. In the first place the more friendly they get with the client the more uncomfortable they feel bringing the subject round to business. And when they do get around to discussing anything resembling business there often isn't any deal to be had. It's either gone to someone else or wasn't available in the first place.

Chasing clients for endless meetings or networking on a social basis both miss the point of real rapport-building, which is that it's not just about the amount of time you spend with someone but the way you spend your time with them.

## MAKING CONNECTIONS

Building rapport is about making a connection with another person. But how do we do this? Most of us know some of what it takes. We know we have to listen, be polite and respond appropriately. But beyond this most people have very little idea of what's involved.

In fact, rapport happens on several levels, and the words we use have less impact than we think they do, compared with our body language, actions and expressions.

Although there have been many studies on the subject of rapport, the landmark one was done by Albert Mehrabian in 1981. He measured the impact of voice tone and body language on our perception of trustworthiness of other people. This showed that if what you are saying and what you are doing conflict, we are most likely to take the message from your body language as more significant. For instance, to put it very simply, if you smile warmly at someone while saying, 'I don't like you', then the other person is unlikely to believe what you say. In the same way, if you frown and glower angrily while saying, 'I love you', they won't believe you either. Your body language will have overruled your words.

What Mehrabian found was that:

- **53 per cent of the impression you make on another person comes from your behaviour and body language**
  The way you act, move, gesture and express yourself; the tone and inflection of your voice. Whether you appear confident, organised, interested. Whether you fumble around, are nervous or distracted. Whether the meaning and point of your message is clear or muddled.
- **40 per cent of the impression you make comes from who you are**
  This means your credibility and competence. Are you likeable, funny, interesting? Are you who you say you are? Do they like you?
- **7 per cent of the impression you make comes from the actual words you say**
  This includes the content of what you are saying, as well as your choice of words.

So much for working out the perfect thing to say. Of course words are important, but when you're building rapport with another person it's vital to pay attention to your body language and to what you do, how you look and the way you present yourself.

Sometimes it's obvious: would you buy a fitness pro-gramme from a very unfit and overweight person? Probably not. But more often it's not so obvious; we gather impressions of another person without being consciously aware of why we make the judgements we make. We walk away thinking, I like him, or, I don't like him, but if asked why we might not be able to relate this to anything he said.

## THE INSIDER'S GUIDE TO RAPPORT

So far you know what doesn't work and you know how important body language and the way you present yourself are. Now it's time to look at four key skills involved in building rapport. Once you know and understand these skills you can apply them in any situation and greatly increase your chances of making a real and effective connection with the other person.

### 1. Pay Attention

This one sounds obvious, but it's not as easy as it sounds. Paying attention is more than sitting upright, face forward with a polite expression.

Really paying attention requires a certain generosity of spirit as well as a good level of physical energy. It means being willing to take in and understand what the person is saying, without waiting to get your own point across or butt in. It's about holding back the desire to judge quickly before you really understand. When your attention is focused, you're giving the other person what they deserve. Do your best not to fake it.

Here are some things you can do to help yourself pay attention:

### Practise

Experts claim our attention spans are getting shorter and shorter but it's something you can improve with practice. Think of it as a muscle and get rid of the flab! Choose to pay full attention to someone, or something, for a few minutes at a time every day, and increase the time. The world is full of distractions and it's often difficult to tell the difference between quality attention and just having your brain filled with details. You'll notice when you're paying attention – it's a little tiring, but such a treat. A bit like a proper meal instead of junk food – you can tell the difference long after you've eaten it.

### Look for a Plus

This simply means entering the conversation with the intention of finding something you like about the other person. A wise friend once said to me, when I was complaining about having to attend another cocktail party, 'Juliet, there is something interesting about everyone – find it.' Whether you know someone well or not, listen as if you've never met them before.

### Shift

If you're having trouble paying attention during a conversation or meeting try shifting your posture. If you pay attention to yourself you'll notice that you have two or three 'postures' you always choose. When we use the one we're most comfortable with it's harder for us to be alert. Try another one – sometimes a little shift can make a big difference to your attention span.

### Meet Your Needs

Is the room stuffy? Do you need more light? Do you need refreshments? A break? Check that you feel comfortable because it's almost impossible to pay attention when you're tired or physically uncomfortable in some way.

If you're thirsty, cold, hot or need to go to the loo then do something about it. I've known people sit through a meeting because they didn't want to take a comfort break. Trouble is afterwards that's about all they remember.

### Make a Connection

Imagine how the other person must be feeling and find an analogy or experience in your own life. Get the message into your heart rather than just your head.

### Take Your Time

Someone once said to me, 'Remember, you have time,' and I've never forgotten it. I often repeat it to myself because it's true, no matter how you feel or what the circumstances.

Allow 20 per cent more time for paying attention than you think is necessary. You may need to put aside what you want to say in order to give full attention to what the other person has to say. Don't allow the pressure of time or your own impatience to make you rush things.

### Check your Conclusions

Check whether the conclusions you're drawing are based on fact or your interpretation of what you're hearing. Ask for more if you're not sure and repeat the other person's key concerns using the words they have used.

Paying attention takes effort, so if you're tired or ill, say so and arrange to meet another time. Giving someone else your attention is a way of treating them, and yourself, with real respect. It honours both of you and they will know whether you are genuine. It can't be faked.

## 2. Learn to Mirror

Let's move on to the third dimension of how we build rapport. Mirroring is something we all do daily with friends and family without even being aware that we do it. By becoming consciously aware of the power of mirroring you can use it to build genuine connections with the people you want to influence.

Mirroring is all about body language, that vital set of signals we send to another person using postures and gestures. It's the natural consequence when people feel comfortable and at ease with one another. As we mirror another person we engage more easily with them, whether they're feeling good or angry or sad.

Think about the signals you send out and the ways you adjust your posture and gestures when you're with another person. If you're comfortable with the person you will adopt a similar position to theirs. For instance if they're sitting and you're standing you might feel awkward, so you sit, too. If they have their head tilted slightly to one side you too may do this, instinctively. This is what mirroring is all about – our instinctive ability to match the pose and gestures of another person when we feel at ease with them.

If someone makes you feel uncomfortable then things are quite different. You may adopt a very different pose to theirs, in order to make it clear that you don't feel a bond. You may be tense, cross your legs, fold your arms or look away. The power of body language, as we know, is immense. And mirroring is the language the body uses to convey messages to another person. Think about a situation where you want to make eye contact with someone across a crowded room. If it's not returned you get the picture – they don't want to know. And if it is, you know pretty quickly that there's the potential for a relationship.

Look around you in a restaurant and notice how people

are sitting together. You will probably be able to tell immediately who has rapport because the people who have it will tend to be holding themselves in the same kind of body postures. They may hold their heads in a similar way, or make gestures of a similar size. A recent study stated that mirroring bonded two people more instantly and effectively than anything else. Imagine two people flirting in a bar. If one leans forward to say something intimate, the other leans in to meet them. If one sits back to take a drink and look the other in the eye the other will do the same.

Mirroring is not about copying or mimicking someone. Natural mirroring is complementary. In other words if you mirror someone you like them and want to get on with them.

Mirroring is a fantastically useful tool to use when building rapport. Once you know how it works you can use it in all kinds of situations to create ease, harmony and good connections. When you mirror effectively it will allow communication to flow far better and the other person won't even be aware that you are putting in conscious effort. They will simply feel that you are on a similar wavelength and will enjoy the exchange with you.

### The Mirroring Exercise

To learn to use mirroring as a communication tool you need to be aware of how you use it and then put in some practice.

Try sitting with someone you know well and mirroring, without mentioning to them what you're doing. Keep it simple and don't mirror gesture for gesture, just adopt a similar body posture to the other person.

Now gently shift your body posture to something very different from the other person. Notice how that feels and what happens next. The conversation will almost certainly change or even end at this point.

When I run this exercise in a room full of people it's

wonderful to watch how each couple takes on a life of its own. It's like seeing lots of individual little movies going on as the couples try different styles of mirroring.

It's useful to remember that as you become more consciously aware of what you do naturally you may initially feel a bit clumsy or strange. But after a little practice this will pass and you'll feel an increased level of confidence, knowing that you can use mirroring as a useful tool to help you establish rapport.

## 3. Match Your Voice

We can also establish rapport with others by matching their voice tone and volume. This is another thing we do naturally and can choose to do consciously to improve communication and build rapport.

Notice the way you use your voice. If someone speaks softly to you, then you will probably lower the level of your own voice. In the same way, if someone is loud you may become louder while speaking to them. If someone shouts at us our instinct is usually to shout back.

When someone refuses to match your tone and volume it can be disconcerting. A friend of mine felt furious with her partner and approached him to discuss why she was so angry. She spoke loudly and quickly but his response was to speak slowly and quietly. Instead of feeling calmed she felt patronised and became even angrier. She needed him to acknowledge her anger through his own tone and volume.

Body language is an important part of voice modulation. If you're going to be loud it will help to stand up. If you want to sound soft it will help to relax your shoulders.

An American client of mine told me that he once shared an office with a Japanese colleague who would stand up, speak quietly and even bow while he was talking on the phone to his Japanese clients. He asked his colleague why he bothered to bow while on the phone as his clients couldn't see him. He replied: 'No, they can't see it, but they can hear it.'

This man understood that the gestures and body language we use support our tone of voice. To sound respectful he needed to be physically respectful.

### Pacing and Leading

This is the ability to move a person gently from one state of mind to another, using our body language, gestures and tone of voice.

For instance, by mirroring the body language and voice tone of an angry or upset person, you acknowledge what is important to them. It is then possible to 'lead' them to a calmer state by moderating your voice and changing your posture.

Be aware, though, you can't lead unless you first pace, that is, match the state they are in. Otherwise you'll just annoy them. Imagine you get to work having had a terrible morning. The dog was sick, your car broke down and you discovered your partner's been having an affair. You sound agitated and distressed as you tell all to your work colleague, who smiles sweetly and says in a soothing voice, 'Never mind, how about a cup of coffee?' At this point the coffee may well end up in his lap. A better response would have been to match you by looking concerned and saying in a loud voice, 'That's awful. You must feel so upset.' Only after mirroring you in this way, and establishing rapport, could he begin to lead you to a calmer state.

A colleague of mine recalls having been called to the office of a powerful client who was notorious for his bad moods, directness and short attention span. When she arrived, he was hunched over his desk on the telephone. After a few minutes he looked up at her and didn't seem to remember why she was there. He eventually signalled her in and began firing questions about the status of a current project.

She 'paced' him by staying standing and answering him in the same direct and to-the-point way in which he was speaking. Before long, he asked her to sit down and began talking in a calmer way. By the time the meeting finished thirty minutes later his feet were on the desk and they were laughing and talking about non-business subjects.

Pacing shows that you understand and respect someone's current state of mind. In this way you can establish rapport before subtly leading them to a different state. We'll come back to this subject in chapter 9, 'Sticky Situations'.

### Choose Your Words

It isn't just the tone and volume of our voices that help to build rapport but the actual words we use. Part of building rapport means being able to express yourself in the 'language' of the other person – using the terms or phrases they use and the same level of sophistication.

I remember once watching a technical wizard trying to explain how a computer worked to a group of elderly web-surfers. Unable to understand his complex terms they looked more and more confused. But instead of simplifying his description he repeated it slower and louder. The result? Frustration on both sides.

When you want to communicate an idea or message to someone else you need to move steadily up the 'words rapport' scale, using a more detailed and involved approach as the other person acknowledges at each level that they have understood you.

Here's a guide to the five levels of communication with words that you can use in building rapport:

**Level One:** The basics – this level is like a verbal brochure. It's when you're talking about you and your idea and describing it in your language. At this level most of us get a bit verbose and give too much information. Keep it simple.

**Example:** I am interested in setting up a teen drop-in centre in our neighbourhood. I've got two teenagers myself and they need somewhere to hang out with their friends. I think it would be great to have it located close to the high school. I hope local people will get involved in fund-raising and setting it up.

**Level Two:** Enough about me – what does it mean to you? This is where you outline what your idea actually means to the other person, so that they start to see why it could be interesting for them.

**Example:** There would be a real benefit to our neighbourhood because it would give local teenagers somewhere to go instead of hanging out on the streets. There's been an increase in teenage crime in the past year and this centre might help to reduce that.

**Level Three:** Let's talk about you *and* do it in your language. At this level you may use some of the terms or expressions the other person has used and explain in more personal terms why it may interest them. The idea will begin to make more sense to them and they will listen with more interest.

**Example:** You mentioned that you have a couple of teenage kids. You also said that you and your daughter have an interest in classical music? That's something we're hoping to include at the centre.

**Level Four:** Let's talk about *us*. You may start, where appropriate, to use examples of how the idea would work if your listener became involved. You help the listener to see themselves using your idea or participating.

**Example:** There is a proposal to get the National School of Music to sponsor a programme if the centre gets up and going. Your daughter might really enjoy that. At a similar centre in another city the parents have got involved in setting up a regular concert series for the parents and kids to enjoy. It's really popular.

**Level Five:** Here's where you want to be – the nirvana of rapport-using words. This is where you get to the things that are really important to the other person and that will ultimately motivate and guide their decision: their values and beliefs.

**Example:** This centre will be a practical and fun way to make a big and lasting difference in the lives of young people. Every child is welcome – from all walks of life. The only rules are no drugs or alcohol, and fun is mandatory! I have had so many parents tell me that getting involved with a centre brought them closer to their teenager. It's really about bringing a sense of community into the life of young people.

## YOUR RAPPORT CHECKLIST

So now you've got all the tools and you're ready to set out for that all-important meeting and to build rapport with the person whose input or decision means so much to you. How will you know you're getting it right? How can you tell whether the other person is bored silly or really interested in what you are saying?

Here are a couple of checklists that you can use as a basic guide to their responses.

If things are going well you might notice any of the following signs in your listener:

- Eyes open, alert, clear, pupils expanded
- Face is expressive
- Facial complexion is bright, not pale
- Overall gestures and body movement animated and open
- They may lean in with enthusiasm, smile or create a feeling of warmth

- Good eye contact with you
- Voice alive, not routine, dull or flat
- Nods head up and down at appropriate times
- Comments are relevant and responsive
- Introduces new relevant and responsive ideas
- Builds on your ideas
- Asks relevant questions
- Says, 'I understand, agree, like'
- Willing to come back or meet again
- Gives prompt, thoughtful responses
- Refers you to others

If it's not going so well these are the signs you might notice in the other person:

- Eyes antagonistic, pupils narrow
- Face is set hard
- Red or pink with anger, or pale
- Animated, but antagonistic, tense, stiff or nervous
- Leans in to challenge
- Has a challenging, stubborn tone
- Eye contact minimal
- Voice alive but tone unfriendly
- Nods head side to side
- Comments opposed
- Introduces opposed ideas
- Asks aggressive questions
- Says, 'I don't agree, don't like'
- Leaves early
- Unwilling to come back
- Reluctant to make a next step

Allow everyone a chance to have one or two things wrong. Maybe they seem very tense or can't sit still. But the rule of thumb is that if you see three bad things happening you could be in trouble. And if you see three things look more closely and the chances are you'll see seven or eight things going wrong!

## WHEN IT WORKS

When you have success in building rapport with another person it feels great. That connection between two people that makes things run smoothly, work well and move forward is more valuable than anything else you can have.

Make yourself familiar with the skills of rapport-building and practise them until you can use them comfortably and easily in any situation. Keep a mental checklist of the skills you need to build rapport and run through them before any important situation. They'll be your greatest ally and give you the advantage when you need it most.

# 4

# THE STYLE GUIDE

*Style is effectiveness of assertion*
**GEORGE BERNARD SHAW**

Why is it that we get along so much more easily with some people than with others? There are people we feel rapport with in a matter of minutes. There's no effort involved; we just 'click' with them and the relationship gets off to a great start.

The answer is style: their style matches our style and we immediately 'understand' one another. Style is like a surfboard that you use to ride each other's wavelength.

If you're naturally easy-going and laid-back then you'll get on with someone else whose style is similar. Whatever your style, whether you're quiet, outspoken or cheerfully sociable, you'll almost certainly get on better with someone whose style matches or fits with yours.

So, what is our 'style'? Whether we realise it or not we all have a set of behaviours that are considered 'typical' of us. Our friends and family know about them, even when we don't. They're familiar with our most common responses and ways of behaving.

Our personal style is based on these usual behaviours and will carry through to our working lives, too. Of course, we don't stick to just one style the whole time. Even the most direct and forceful personality will have laid-back, easy-going moments. But each of us has a style that is predominant and will come across most often. So, while it's not a good idea to put everyone you know into boxes, it can be useful to know which style you identify with most clearly and the styles of those you need to communicate with.

Doing this will give you a head start. Once you know how to identify styles you can build rapport with people who are not at all like you. It might not come naturally, as it does with someone of a similar style, but with a little effort you can still make it happen.

Instead of jarring with someone whose style is very different, you can work with them, know what to expect from them and respond in ways you know they will understand and connect with. In other words you will be better able to mirror, match, pace and lead.

This chapter is a guide to the main behaviour styles you will come across. As you read through the descriptions you'll probably recognise yourself and most of the people you know. It's great fun and can also be very helpful. When you're in new or demanding situations you'll be able to recognise the styles of the people involved. Then you can use your inside knowledge to build rapport, persuade and influence.

People have been recognising and using styles for thousands of years. In fact, some of the available information about styles comes from sources as far back as Hippocrates in 400 BC.

The version I'm going to give you is my own take on the style principle, based on many years of working with people and made up of a blend of approaches, in particular the one we used during my twelve years with Rogen International.

## THE FOUR KEY STYLES

We all fall into one of four key styles and these are

1. Direct
2. Analytical
3. Social
4. Expressive

Let's go through them one at a time. I'll give you the main characteristics of each one before going on to show you what you can do to build rapport with someone who displays that particular style.

### 1. Direct

This is the attitude of the direct person:

Please get to the point as soon as you can. Time is important to me and I don't like people who waffle. Promise me early in the meeting that you will stick to the agreed timing and then do it.

I like it when you tell me what you want at the beginning of the meeting. Don't make me wait because I can usually tell what you are going to say anyway. I have a short attention span. I like control and I'll take it if I see you're not doing so fairly early on. You'll know I'm losing interest when I ask you to hand me any papers you've brought with you so that I can look through them and take the meeting in the direction I choose. If it's a presentation I'll flip through anything you've given me while you're talking. I'll probably start to squirm around in my chair if you're not getting to the points. I may even sigh loudly. I may also start to look at my watch – sooner than you expect.

I will ask you direct questions from early on in the meeting and I'll expect you to give me well-prepared, brief answers to my questions. I probably won't give you a long meeting so be prepared to cut to the salient points. I'm usually a decision-maker so be sure I know what you want from me or those who work with me. If you don't know, say you don't know. I am usually calm, controlled, formal and orderly.

Small talk usually doesn't impress me. I respect focus and clarity. I can come across as gruff and curt sometimes, but stick with me – I need to hear good ideas and I like smart, interested and enthusiastic people as much as the next person.

My answering machine message will also be brief and will say something like 'You have reached . . . please leave your name and number.' That's it.

### How do you recognise one?

- Environment is tidy and organised
- Impatient
- Questions and answers short, pointed, precise
- Little if any small talk
- Likes specific evidence
- Responds well to confrontation
- Energetic, forceful

### To build rapport with the direct person

- Be punctual
- Keep the meeting short
- Be prepared for every possible eventuality and question
- Start with the point or outcome you want
- Use evidence or back-up that is very specific and factual
- Make your message or presentation well-structured

- Be able to answer questions in a direct, brief and decisive way
- Make your questions incisive – show that you know what you're talking about
- Don't bother with small talk or try to be too friendly
- If you write a letter, state what you want in the first brief paragraph, including any next steps you may have discussed

I have a client whose firm I have worked with for ten years. Our relationship, which is good, constructive and on-going, consists of an annual five-minute phone conversation. That's what he wants, that's what he gets. It is enough for him. My preference would be to talk to him more, to meet, chat, get friendly. But he's a direct person and for him the five minutes is perfect.

## 2 Analytical

This is the attitude of the analytical person:

I'm usually on time and fairly disciplined. I like technical and logical challenges. You may see charts and graphs in my office and when I describe things I may do it with lines, arrows and continuums.

I love detail. It's a good idea to find out who I am in advance and to send me details of what we'll discuss before we meet. I enjoy the process of hearing about how you did what you did because it helps me to understand you and decide whether what you're saying has merit. If your method is well-thought-through, then your idea has a good chance of getting my go-ahead. If you've messed up on the detail I'll eat you alive.

I will give you the time you need to get through your argument. I may divert you sometimes because I want a detailed answer to some aspect of what you are telling me. Don't dismiss me; just give me a good answer that satisfies me you have thought this through. Your safest bet is to build your argument for me step by step, showing me your thinking or workings at each stage.

I don't respond well to a direct approach and I'm not influenced by bravado. One other point: I like to consider things, so I may take a bit longer to make a decision.

My answering machine message might say: 'Good morning. You have reached the voicemail of . . . on Thursday 16th of June 2004. I am not at my desk at the moment but I will return at 3 p.m. If you would like to leave a message, do so after the beep – leaving your name, phone number, time of call and the reason you are calling. I will get back to you as soon as possible.'

### How do you recognise one?

- Environment is tidy and organised
- Questions and answers are precise, pointed and technical
- Keeps emotional issues out of small talk; likely to say, 'How was the traffic?' rather than, 'How are you feeling?'
- Logical, fact-oriented
- Will ask for supporting data, details and sources

### To build rapport with the analytical person

- Be on time and have your information clearly ordered and ready to go
- Be pointed and technical
- Don't rush the pace, take your time
- Support your answers to questions with as much evidence as possible, preferably two or three types of evidence
- Be low-key in your style – careful, sincere and orderly without too much enthusiasm or bounce
- Don't use words such as intuitive, think, believe, feel, etc.
- Do use words such as rational, know, prove, demonstrate, analyse, etc.

I had a client who was so biased towards the analytical that he would only ever approve an idea if it was presented to him in a certain way. Everyone who worked with him learned to give him the detail he insisted on. This meant that first you had to explain how you came to the idea and your thinking behind it. Then you had to present any tests or insights you had found to reinforce your thinking. Finally you could come to the idea itself. Approach him any other way and you'd be sent back to the drawing board. He had to know the background before he would understand or believe the idea. He also had to have each major issue explained in at least two ways – with the evidence to back them up.

## 3. Social

This is the attitude of the social person:

If I'm late for a meeting it's because I was looking after someone or trying to resolve a conflict or problem. I really like to get involved in the personal, emotional and human side of things.

I don't like friction. I'm proud of my relationships and friends and people describe me as warm, supportive and patient. I like balance and harmony. I enjoy it when you make friendly small talk with me.

I can be very politically astute. I like meetings and sometimes I attend them even when I am not essential to the objective. People rely on me to understand the 'softer' issues and invite me to come along to get a 'read' on the situation. I sometimes have a lot of influence in an organisation. I can be very important to a decision-maker and have their ear.

If I'm a decision-maker, I'm interested in what it would be like to work with you. I want to know how everyone feels about things before I make my decision. I may have family photographs around me, as well as drawings, colourful paintings and inspirational sayings. People issues are very important to me so I'll be looking to see whether you'll fit into the team and get along with the others in the organisation.

A successful meeting to me is one where we may not get to the objective; the most important thing is that we build rapport. I won't mind scheduling another meeting to get to the business side of things. I don't like confrontation very much so you might not know exactly how I feel about something when the meeting ends.

My answering machine message might say: 'Hello, you have reached . . . I'm sorry I'm not here to take your call. Please leave your name and number and I will get back to you as soon as possible. I look forward to speaking to you soon. Goodbye and thanks.'

### How do you recognise one?

- Environment relaxed, family photos around
- Questions and answers are usually based on how others think and feel or may be affected
- Likes plenty of small talk
- Dislikes being rushed or pushed into a decision
- Usually avoids confrontation

### To build rapport with the social person

- If you're late, have a good people reason
- Be warm, friendly and talkative
- Don't rush; go at a relaxed pace. Avoid a sense of urgency
- Wait to begin the business side of things until the other person indicates that they are ready
- Show that you are aware of how others will be affected by what you are proposing
- Talk about your personal experience, where relevant

- Your personal promise will be more important than statistical back-up or factual evidence

I have a client who was known for looking after his team better than anyone else in his organisation. Everyone wanted to be on his team because it was a sure way to do the sort of work you wanted to do and have fun. They often socialised together and had a wonderful camaraderie.

I made a classic error with this man. I can be pretty direct and I inadvertently upset one of his team members when we were working late at night on a high-pressure presentation. The following day the client came back to me yelling at the top of his voice and very upset about how I had done this to his colleague. After he'd vented his anger I apologised and later in the day went to the person I'd upset with chocolates, flowers and an apology. After that, this client and I were great friends. He was satisfied that I'd put things right and I knew exactly which approach to use with him and his team.

## 4. Expressive

This is the attitude of the expressive person:

I am considered to be a good communicator – not necessarily clear, but expressive and open and with lots of energy. I often have my ego tied up in what I say, so be careful about how you respond. It's best to hear me out. When you do respond, I like it when you have a creative way to explain what you mean. I don't like process very much – don't bother with detailed explanations. I have a tendency to think in terms of the big picture so paint a picture of the final result for me, with lots of colourful description and adjectives. I like to feel inspired and excited.

Expect some personal questions. My small talk will be personal and positive. I can be recognised by my high energy, animation and intuitive approach. I'm excitable so make sure we have an agreement, not just an adrenaline-fuelled session.

I may also jump around in my thinking, and you might get lost, so make sure you can keep up. I tend to be judgemental and easily bored. If you're not creative or emotional I may think you're dull.

I'm likely not to have an answering machine message. If I do then someone else has recorded it for me, or it will be brief.

### How do you recognise one?

- Environment colourful and slightly disorganised
- Will ask creative questions and seek creative answers
- Likes positive personal small talk
- Likes to be entertained
- Excitable, articulate, animated
- May take things personally
- Hates detail

### To build rapport with the expressive person

- Be on time
- Be confident and dynamic
- Be warm, creative and colourful
- Don't compete
- Bring in the big picture early in the meeting, then use the rest of the meeting to bring the picture to life
- Keep detail to a minimum
- Keep pace with what the other person is thinking and saying

A major advertising-agency client of mine was so expressive that his meetings were almost theatrical. When he spoke his gestures were big, his voice full and loud, his language descriptive and colourful. During meetings, while others were talking, he would often wander slowly around the room, rubbing the shoulders of his team members who were seated, pausing while standing over the person speaking. He would also occasionally lie on the floor at the back of the room to rest or read the newspaper, much to the dismay of whoever was talking. He was highly creative and got away with this most of the time because he was so successful. Some of his clients found it amusing, but others found it egotistical and rude. Whichever way you took him, he was slightly mad – and a classic example of an extreme expressive.

## LOOK FOR CLUES

You'll often find that someone seems to be a combination of two styles. Some direct people are very expressive, too, and vice versa. In the same way, some analytical people can also be very direct or quite social. Some combinations don't work, though. Analytical types are rarely if ever expressive, and social types are rarely direct.

Because it isn't always obvious which type or mix of types someone is, take your time and look for clues when assessing how to approach them.

I had a client who seemed to be a clear social type. He was friendly, warm and chatty and he liked to spend plenty of time on personal conversation before getting down to business.

Because of this I made my approach to him very social, concentrating on the people and human aspects of the presentation. Mistake! I'd missed some obvious clues, such as the detailed charts on his walls, and soon realised that when it came to business this very sociable man was, in fact, highly analytical. He wanted detail, evidence and facts – and plenty of them. I had to go back and redo my proposal, making it far more analytical, before we could do business.

Recognising someone's style isn't a guarantee that things

will go well. But it will give you a double advantage. First you'll feel more confident and in control. And second, you'll have a clearer idea of how to respond to them in a way that will help you build rapport and reach the outcome you want.

# 5
# MAKING YOUR MESSAGE PERSUASIVE

*Nothing is more terrible than activity without insight*
**THOMAS CARLYLE**

Now that you know how to build rapport with the person you are communicating with it's time to look in more detail at the message you want to put across. How are you going to make your message really stand out? What will set it apart from others? What will make the person receiving your message think, This is different, I like this, or I want this?

Having rapport with the other person is an essential first step. Rapport is an on-going process, but when you've established the initial rapport you're on your way. However, if your message is unclear, boring, unoriginal, irrelevant or too long, then you'll lose the ground you've gained, fall flat on your face and chip away at any rapport you have established.

That's why this chapter is about making your message really persuasive. To deliver a message that is unbeatable, original and goes straight to the point of what your listener wants to hear, you need to know how to turn information into insight, how to trim the fat from your message and how to strengthen its muscle. The most important thing to know when you set out to make your message persuasive is that its content needs to reflect what your listener wants. Too many people make the mistake of simply talking to themselves. They put together a message that they think is great, but what they haven't done is consider whether the other person will think it's great.

When you deliver a message the other person will be thinking, Why should I believe you? What's in this for me, or my company? Why should I choose you and not the other person who has a similar idea or approach?

If you're going to answer these questions and deliver a message that is relevant and successful you must consider, in as much detail as possible, who the other person is and what they want. Your message must tell them exactly how they'll benefit from what you have to offer.

To create a perfectly honed, fine-tuned message which does exactly what you want it to there are three steps:

1. Find out as much as you can about the person or people you are going to present your message to
2. Determine what is important to them and what will influence their decision about you and your idea
3. Build a persuasive message based on what you learned in the previous two steps

If you follow these three steps your message will be on-target, well defined and perfectly tuned to fit the person you're going to present it to. So, let's go into a bit more detail about what's involved in each step.


## STEP ONE: FIND OUT AS MUCH AS YOU CAN ABOUT THE PERSON OR PEOPLE YOU ARE GOING TO PRESENT YOUR MESSAGE TO

You can't possibly make your message meaningful without knowing something about the person who will receive it.

Don't put yourself into the situation of trying to persuade someone you don't know. If you do that you're just guessing what they want, and you may well guess wrong. Presenting to someone you know nothing about is like feeling around in the dark for something you want. You may find it, but you probably won't.

The strongest way to differentiate yourself is by knowing your listeners better than anyone else knows them. That way you can work out how to make your message meaningful to them.

To begin with you need to find some basic information about the person you will meet and their organisation. This isn't as hard as it may seem. There are all kinds of ways of gathering information, if you're prepared to put in a little effort and to be resourceful. Going the extra mile at this stage can make the difference between failure and success.

Here are some of the questions you may want to find answers to. Pick the ones that seem most relevant to your situation and add more if you think of them.

## The person

- What is this person's preferred listening style? Are they direct and to the point, energetic and dynamic or quiet and reserved?
- What is their work background, social background, education level?
- How much do you know about what they do? About their business?
- Are there any local customs or prejudices to be aware of?
- What issues are really important to them right now?
- What do they want?
- What do they need?
- Whose opinion do they respect?

- What are they proud of or loyal to?
- What excites them? Gets them really interested?
- What ideas, feelings or experiences do you have in common?

## Your meeting with them

- How much do they know about you? About your idea? What is their attitude towards you?
- What are they expecting from you – a presentation? A chat? A formal meeting?
- Will anything affect when you meet? Is timing important?
- What should you not say?

## The business considerations

- Who are their competitors and how will what you are suggesting help them gain an advantage over them?
- Have you accommodated the politics in their organisation?
- Can you make it clear to them how you are different from others who may be offering them something? How can you help them achieve their objectives?
- Can they act now, even if they do like your idea?
- How much are they prepared to spend? Have they spent money on this kind of thing before?
- Who signs the cheque?
- Who has the power to say no?
- Who has the most to lose from your idea succeeding?

## The decision

- How do they make decisions? What criteria will they use? Who else is involved?
- Who is responsible for making the decision?
- How much time and information do they need to make a decision?

97

- What else might influence their decision? Someone? Something?
- What do you think the most important consideration will be in their decision?

OK, that's a lot of information. And you may have come up with more questions of your own, depending on the situation you will be in and the person or people you will deal with.

So, where do you get all this information?

Well, the first thing to say is that no matter how daunting or difficult it may seem you can always find at least some of the information you want. There is always a way. Keep looking. Ask, ask, ask. Be creative. There are many different ways of gathering information and whatever you are able to find out will give you something to build on and put you in a stronger position.

Here are some of the sources of information you can try:

## Other People

You can find out a lot by talking to people who know the person you will be meeting. You may also be able to talk to people in the organisation, or those who will be in the meeting with you.

You'd be surprised how much information is out there. Be brave about asking; I've seen so many people prepared to assume rather than risk the embarrassment of asking. Of course you must tread carefully – you don't want to offend anyone by prying.

Use an open, honest approach and be discreet. Don't get dragged into gossiping. One of the best approaches is to say that you have organised a meeting with so-and-so and you would like to fill in some information gaps in order to make the meeting more relevant for them.

## The Internet

Most businesses, corporations and organisations, even very small ones, have a website that you can access for information. This may not tell you a lot about the person you will meet, but you will be able to gather clues about the type of organisation it is and its aims and ethos.

## Reports

If it is a business or organisation you are going to you can ask for copies of their last few annual reports, or any other reports that have been written about them. For instance, if it was a school you could look at their school inspector's Ofsted reports.

## Newspapers

Old newspaper reports can be very useful. Something as simple as going to the local library to read up on background information can help you to feel better prepared. Read relevant articles and highlight important points that you can use.

## The Horse's Mouth

One of the most overlooked and best places to go for information is from the person you are going to meet. This is not always possible but, depending on the situation, you may be able to ask for a quick chat ahead of the meeting or to arrange to get together more informally first.

Use any or all of these sources of information to put together as clear and full a picture as possible of the person you will present your message to and what they want. This kind of preparation is invaluable and will help you to clearly define and direct your message.

This story is a wonderful example of how doing a little unofficial homework can make all the difference:

I worked on a job in Los Angeles that involved my clients, an advertising agency, pitching to the head of one of the big Hollywood studios. This woman had a fearsome reputation. She was known as a tyrant who was tough, demanding and liked to embarrass people in meetings. Especially men. The panel pitching from the agency was all-male and they were terrified just thinking about meeting her. But we did our homework. We found someone who had been friends with her since childhood. They gave us some information that didn't invade her privacy but was enough to calm the pitch team.

To set against her reputation for slaying men in meetings we found out that:

- She adored home-made chocolate chip cookies with pecans in them
- She dabbled in watercolour painting
- She had two big fat cats called Chewy and Chunky
- She spent a lot of her spare time working with a charity for disadvantaged inner-city kids

Suddenly we didn't have a dragon lady, we had a creative, compassionate and intelligent woman with a sense of humour.

When the time came for the pitch we were ready. We had the cookies, freshly baked, ready for the tea break. We had some of the illustrations done in watercolour. She loved them and asked to keep some. She and our designer swapped stories about art school.

We also included a recommendation for community follow-up as part of the pitch, including an option to do gratis work for her charity.

Everyone relaxed, which helped the pitch immensely. We enjoyed it, she enjoyed it and, yes, my clients won the business.

## STEP TWO: DETERMINE WHAT IS IMPORTANT TO THEM AND WHAT WILL INFLUENCE THEIR DECISION ABOUT YOU AND YOUR IDEA

So, now you have some interesting information about the person to whom you will deliver your message and their organisation.

The next step is to work out how to position your message, based on what you know. Your listener will be making a decision to be persuaded or influenced by you, rather than by something or someone else. What will influence this decision is what is important to your listener and what motivates them.

Think about yourself when you have to make a decision about something. Sometimes the decision is easy because it is clear-cut, the option has everything you want and it 'does the job'. That is, it meets your criteria or needs exactly. Say you're looking for a new fridge and you find one that is the size you want, the colour you want and a good price. Deal done.

At other times a decision can be a little less clear. For example, you might find a fridge that is a fantastic bargain and a great colour but doesn't quite fit the space you have in mind for it in your kitchen. Are you going to take the time and trouble to enlarge the space, or give this fridge a miss in the hopes of finding one that's also a perfect fit? No amount of talking and cajoling on the part of a salesperson will convince you if your criteria aren't being met.

There are many factors at work when we make a decision. The experts have classified things that motivate us into three categories: Rational, Emotional and Political/Cultural.

### Rational
Rational motivations concern the practical and technical aspects of a decision. These might include cost, efficiency,

whether someone can deliver on time, whether a product is made of the right materials and whether it will do the job. Rational motivations are about ticking off the boxes on a checklist.

## Emotional

Emotional motivations are a little hazier. They relate to our ego or emotions and will concern the feeling aspects of a decision. Someone making an emotional decision will go on whether they like the other person and whether it feels right.

## Political/Cultural

Political/cultural motivations usually refer to a person's sense of power and safety in an organisation or a unit. These will concern whether the person feels they will look good, achieve more power, or forward their ambitions.

Now let's take these general motivations and set them alongside the specific motivations of the person you want to influence. In other words, put the information you gathered in step one together with these considerations and you will create a fuller, clearer picture of what you need to address in your message.

One of the most important aspects you need to consider is what the sphere of influence is of the person you will deliver your message to. At what level do they operate, if they are part of an organisation? At every level there are specific factors which will influence the way they see you and the decision they make about you and what you have to offer.

For instance, a chief executive will be considering the big picture and their strategy for the future. They'll be concerned with public relations, shareholder perception and company performance. But a sales director will be more concerned with targets and budgets, the market share and the competition, new business and the company's products, while a human resources manager will be looking at getting the best people, training, new ideas for employee satisfaction and work-life balance.

You can make your own list of the position-related factors likely to influence the person or people you are going to meet. Think about what that person is going to be concerned about, who they must answer to and what they must deliver as part of their job.

Even in a non-business context this will apply. For instance, say you want to persuade someone to take part in your sponsored run. It will help if you think about who they are, what matters to them and what outcome they might want. You can then address these factors when you approach them. For one person, raising money for charity might be the most important factor, while for another, it would be getting fit. Of course, you can't always know the answers to what motivated a person to make a decision, but doing your homework in advance can definitely put the odds in your favour and make a huge difference to the outcome of your efforts.

I worked with a client recently who won a contract to provide a new information-service technology to a large organisation. The challenge was that he had to 'sell' it to the various users throughout the organisation. Each user group would then decide what the benefits were for them and how they would use it.

He began by trying to talk to everyone at once about all the things they could do with his service. But after a short while he realised he wasn't getting anywhere. His meetings were taking too long and people weren't turning up.

He realised that each user in the organisation wanted something different. The chief executive wanted a brief overview, something in writing that he could digest like a newspaper in ten minutes in the morning. The human resources manager wanted to download various employee-related issues on to their brand-new intranet service to attract more employees to their site. The sales department wanted something they could talk to their clients about and the finance director didn't care what it was all about, he just wanted to be sure that they weren't spending more than they needed to.

Different things matter to different people. My client decided he could hasten the take-up of his service by giving individual presentations aimed at the specific needs of the different departments. It worked.

## STEP THREE: BUILD A PERSUASIVE MESSAGE BASED ON WHAT YOU LEARNED IN THE PREVIOUS TWO STEPS

Now it's time to look at the content of your message in the light of the research that you've done. Let's take this in three stages.

### 1. Spell out the Benefits

The first consideration for anyone listening to your message is going to be: 'How will I benefit from what you are proposing?'

It is no good going into lots of detail or telling a story if it isn't relevant to the person listening. The test is to ask yourself: What will this person be able to have that they don't have now, to do better or to become as a result of my idea? What's in it for them?

Sometimes it's hard to separate explaining the process of what you do from the outcome. But most people aren't particularly interested in the process. If you want to get to what's in it for them, focus on the outcome.

We often overlook telling people what is in it for them. It seems so obvious, you might think. Yet it isn't. Of course, your listener could probably make the leap and work it out for themselves. But don't make people work too hard because they won't. And besides, even if they do get to it themselves, you will powerfully reinforce it by stating it clearly as part of your message.

Use phrases such as 'This is important to you because . . .', 'This means to you that . . .', 'You should care because . . .', or 'Here's what it means to you . . .' When you talk like this your listener will feel personally involved and will become interested.

Here is a good example of this. Marcia built a successful foundation for educating disabled children. Even though she was really busy, she managed over the years to keep her weekends free to spend time with her husband and two children. One day she was approached by the Government to become involved in developing a special-education council, which would mean that she would be working full-time and travelling a lot, including at weekends. She needed her husband's support on this because he would be left alone with the children a few days a month. When Marcia was explaining the new job to him she talked about how the new council would improve the lives of so many young people and families across England. Her husband appreciated this, but still felt rather put out about the whole thing. What Marcia had forgotten to talk about was how her husband might benefit personally. When she realised this she told him that the job would pay for babysitters more often and would include four weeks' paid leave each year so that they could take the sailing holiday they had dreamed of. Needless to say, her husband was a lot happier to lend his support after this.

## 2. Say Less not More
A lot of people and firms throw all kinds of information at potential clients, and each other, when they pitch for new

business. They act on the principle that more is better, believing that if they throw everything in, something will stick. Not the case. The result is likely to be that the client is bored, irritated or worn out and can't wait to show them the door before the pitch is even finished. I've had clients tell me that the minute someone walks through the door with an armful of documents they feel dread.

This is true whether you're presenting a message at corporate level or going to see the head of the local junior school to ask them to let you organise a book club. The headteacher will want a short, clear discussion just as much as the head of a multinational corporation will.

Whatever level you're working at, the best approach by far is to do your homework so that you can focus on fewer, more refined and relevant details. A few hours spent preparing can be worth their weight in gold.

### 3. Use Evidence and Prove It!

The use of evidence is the final piece of the puzzle, the ah-ha! in your listener's mind. Evidence is information indicating whether something is true or valid. Use whatever it takes and however much of it you need to support what you are saying.

Here are some of the most common types:

**Facts:** make sure they are irrefutable! 'The XYZ Foundation is the only provider of these services to women', 'There are ten reported cases this year in Hollyoaks', or, 'Not one person has visited the site.'

**Statistics:** don't throw in hundreds of statistics; they can be mind-numbing. But a few carefully positioned ones can support your case. For instance: 'X per cent of London homes have television sets', 'The US consumes more fossil fuel as a percentage of population than any other country', 'There are 7 grams of fat in a container of goats' yoghurt.'

**Case Studies or Examples**: use examples to explain who else has done it, what they did and what the results were. For instance: 'X tried this and got y result', or, 'We have used this for two other clients who have benefited in the following ways.'

**Demonstration**: show how your product or idea will work. Demonstrations should be simple and to the point; don't go into endless lists, figures or tables. One clever person I know chose to 'act out' the styles and types of people who would use her product, rather than going through tables of facts. It was entertaining and the users came to life; we all felt we recognised them. So, if you're selling a pen, show your client what it's like to write with it.

**Testimonials**: quote an expert on the subject or someone who has used or experienced it. Industry associations and institutional bodies, as well as popular figures or celebrities, can be used as examples.

**Hypothetical Examples**: these might go along the lines of: 'If you were to invest today, by 2007 it will have grown to . . .' or, 'If we replaced every tree we logged with two trees, we could heal the forest in two years.'

**Visual Aids**: they say a picture is worth a thousand words and it's true. Where appropriate, it's good to 'illustrate' or 'show' someone rather than try to explain it.

**Analogy**: this is a way of explaining something by comparing it to something else. It can make something complicated or obscure become clear. For example: 'There was so much excess stationery that we could have filled this auditorium.'

Remember that evidence is there to help you back up what you are saying. It takes what you say and makes it true for the listener. Different types of evidence appeal to different types of people depending on what you know to be their biases, motivations and understanding.

When you put your evidence together keep in mind the

style of the person you will present it to. For example, a highly analytical person would appreciate a more detailed explanation of something than someone who may be highly artistic or expressive.

I remember sitting in a presentation given by a firm of accountants who were pitching for my firm's business. They were taking a lot of care, showing us how well their technology worked and how their management systems made processing easy and accurate. They even brought along a computer screen to demonstrate it and took us through the intricacies of the process.

The trouble was they hadn't done their homework. I wasn't interested in that aspect of their business or in a lengthy, detailed presentation. I wanted to spend as little time on accounting as possible. All I needed to know was that they could make it easy and fast and not make mistakes. They were detail-oriented and wanted me to come along for the ride but this left me feeling that the relationship would be time-consuming and, frankly, not much fun.

Instead they could have spent the time demonstrating how easy the relationship could be and how little of my time they would need. They might have given examples of how others like me have used them to make their lives easier and testimonials about how they have avoided problems for others.

This firm needed to spell out the benefits in a far simpler way, using evidence to back up what they offered. If they'd done this and helped me see how much fun we'd have working together I'd have snapped them up.

## PUTTING IT ALL TOGETHER

Now you know that to create a really persuasive message you need to put time and effort into the background preparation.

Become a sleuth and find out as much as possible about the person you're going to be meeting.

The next step is to look at the message itself and to structure it in the most effective way possible. In the next chapter I'll show you how to put together a message that goes straight to the point and is entertaining, relevant and very persuasive.

# 6

# STRUCTURING YOUR MESSAGE

*I have never been able to understand why it is that just because I am unintelligible nobody understands me*
**MILTON MAYER**

When you present a message to someone, whether formally, informally, over the phone or in person, the structure of your message is all-important. If you present it in a confused, sloppy or jumbled way then it's unlikely to be understood. The other person will feel impatient, unclear about what you want and may well be unlikely to support or encourage you in the way that you'd like.

Why leave people irritated or puzzled when, with a little effort, you can present your message in a clear and straightforward way that will leave them in no doubt about what you're saying and what you want? Result? You're far more likely to get it.

That's why this chapter is all about structuring your message. In the first part of the chapter we'll look at the basic principles of all structures: how to create a good beginning, choose the steps along the way, deal with transitions and then make an ending with impact. We'll also look at how to help you cut your preparation time in half.

Then we'll go on to look at the different kinds of structures you might use in different situations. For instance, the structure for a short, off-the-cuff speech would be different to the structure for an hour-long formal presentation. With nine basic structures to choose from you'll be able to select the most appropriate one for any situation.

Giving your message a sound structure won't just help your listeners, it will help you too. With a strong structure to work around you'll feel more relaxed and confident, you'll give yourself more flexibility and you'll stay in control. Nothing creates nervousness and loss of control quicker than floundering around in a structureless talk, trying to remember what you've said, where you are and what you still want to say.

Of course, everyone feels nervous when presenting, especially if the result of what you're about to say is very important to you. But structure puts the butterflies diving haphazardly around in your belly into flying formation. Create a good structure and you and your listener will both sigh with relief. No one should have to work too hard to understand what's going on.

Most of us have a good idea of what a written structure should look like. We learn them in school, so producing a written document shouldn't be too hard. But in this chapter we'll be looking mostly at the structures for talks and face-to-face presentations – rather different to the written versions.

For a face-to-face presentation, structure is even more important than it is for a written report or presentation. The reader can flick through the written version, going back to check on things they may not be clear about. But when you're talking, you decide the order in which the listener receives the information and what gets emphasis and priority. They hear it only once, so it needs to be crystal-clear.

## THE CORE COMPONENTS OF ANY FACE-TO-FACE PRESENTATION

These are the things your listeners will expect to hear and that will make it easier for them to remember what you've said:

- Subject: what you are talking about specifically
- Signposts: the areas you'll cover – sometimes known as an agenda
- Body:  the content, where you'll talk in detail about your message – the meat of the matter
- Summary: the reminder, at the end, of key areas of your message
- Conclusion: your point

## PREPARING YOUR PRESENTATION

When we prepare a message, talk or presentation, most of us spend a lot of time trying to come up with the content. We work from the middle out. We say to ourselves, 'Hmm, I know my subject. Now what are all the things I should or could say about it?'

Trouble is, you could go on for ever like that. Here's an approach that will cut your preparation time in half.

So, grab a pen and sit down. . .

1. Before doing anything, decide exactly what your subject is. It is amazing how many people proceed without being absolutely clear about this.
2. Decide what your main point, idea, recommendation or conclusion is. When you've decided on your objective, write it

out in one sentence. It should be clear and precise, without any negatives. A good way to test it is to ask yourself what you want your listeners to do or think as a result of your presentation.

3. Decide which areas of information you need to cover in order to get this message across: your signposts. Keep in mind your conclusion as you list them. Will covering these areas help you achieve it?

You've now determined the three or four most important things to consider or areas you'll need to cover in order to make your point strongly. Most of the work is already done! Always refer back to these signposts as you put the rest of the message together.

Now you can start to collect your content.

4. Put together the content of the body of your presentation by filling in the necessary information under the signposts you've chosen. Again, keep in mind your conclusion/objective and at each step ask yourself, 'Will talking about this specific area lead me to my desired objective?' Anything in your presentation should be there only because it helps you to put your proposal or idea across more clearly and convincingly.

5. Now decide what key summary point or points you'll want to mention as you're wrapping up. At this stage there should be no new information, just the main things you want people to remember.

6. A final tidy up. Go back through your presentation and decide what phrases you can use to make the transitions between your content sections really clear.

7. Decide what administrative remarks, if any, you'll need to make. Check the time you'll have, whether there will be any questions, any introductions required, any handouts that need mentioning, breaks, fire alarm instructions etc.

8. Come up with a way to creatively focus your listeners' attention

at the beginning of your presentation so that they're ready and eager to hear what you have to say.

And that's it! A simple, easy-to-follow and foolproof way of putting together any presentation, no matter how long or short. I'll give you more details about how to create effective beginnings and endings, how to sort out your areas of information, how to focus listeners' attention and how to make smooth transitions in the next few sections.

## THE PRINCIPLES OF STRUCTURE

Whatever kind of structure you use for your talk or presentation, you need to follow certain basic principles. Once you know them you can apply them to anything, whether it's impromptu and informal or prepared well in advance and delivered in a formal setting.

The thing that is true of all face-to-face presentation, is that it works best if you keep in mind a simple principle about communication. People listen and absorb better if you do three things:

1. Beginning: *prepare your listener to receive your message*
2. Middle: *deliver what you said you were going to*
3. Ending: *make sure they have received and understood your message*

### Beginning

Aristotle said, 'The beginning is half of the whole.'

If you can get the beginning right, you stand a far better chance of the rest of your message being delivered well and accepted by your listeners. There are two things you need to do at the beginning that will go a long way towards getting you successfully through to the end:

## 1 Clear their minds of distractions

Just before you begin any presentation you're at your most nervous and your audience is distracted. They may be thinking about the last thing they were doing, what they are going to do afterwards, how long you'll speak for or just chatting to one another. They're not really paying attention to you yet.

To clear their minds of these distractions make whatever administrative remarks are necessary or appropriate. This gets everyone listening, as well as sorting out minor details, such as where the loos are or when the break will be. Introductions and welcomes are made at this stage and you can say whether there will be time for questions at the end.

If the situation is such that you don't need to make administrative remarks you can simply comment on the fact that you're glad to see everyone there, or to be there. And it always helps to acknowledge the amount of time you have. This kind of beginning, whether formal or informal, allows you to have an early exchange of conversation, eye contact and agreement. When it's done naturally and well it relaxes you and everyone else. Now, they're ready for you to begin.

## 2. Creatively focus their attention

This is also known as a creative opening or an opening gambit. The reason why you may choose to do this – and it is optional – is to focus creatively, not get attention. You can get attention by taking off your clothes. Maybe not a good idea unless you're at the opening of a nudist fest.

The important thing about focusing attention is that what you choose needs to be relevant. It can't just be the same old gag you always use or a joke you like. It needs to be something that will prepare the way for what you have to say next, while being entertaining in itself. When it works the audience will be paying attention and looking forward to your next words.

Here are nine great ways to focus attention:

1. **Ask the audience a question:** this is good if you can get the answer you want, or at least an answer you can handle. If the question is not asked well – if it's too rhetorical or obvious, for example – you can get a cheeky answer from someone in the room that may throw you. Then people remember how your question was thrown back in your face, rather than the answer! The other potential problem here is that no one may answer; the audience may be shy or hold back. Be ready to answer the question yourself and move on.

2. **Tell a joke:** be careful with this one because it's a rare joke that doesn't offend someone. Unless you are absolutely sure, don't do it.

3. **Use an anecdote:** this is a very short human-interest story about a real incident or person. These are good because people like to hear stories about people. But make sure it's relevant. I have a client who doesn't speak for more than a few minutes before an anecdote pops out to personalise his subject. He's got lots of tales about the brave soldier or the benevolent person or the dignified grandmother. These always bring nods of recognition from the audience.

4. **Try an aphorism:** a quote or familiar saying can be a good opener. Try to steer clear of the usual suspects though. No offence to Abe Lincoln, Winston Churchill and certain sports coaches but they've been used too many times. There are lots of wonderful books available for ideas.

5. **Talk about a real, dramatic or funny situation:** sometimes relevant stories are right under your nose. These can be a down-to-earth way to make a point. I've had good luck with this by arriving early to client conferences where I'm due to speak and collecting stories about what's been happening

during the conference so far. There's always something relevant to your objective and meaningful to the group to be found.

6. **Use a factoid:** this is a juicy statistic or a little-known fact. I heard about the head of a major consulting firm who starts his presentation to chief executives about economic-growth crisis with a factoid about how 'investors are looking for companies who have double-digit growth. Of the major companies listed here – not one offers near that kind of growth.' By the time he was finished with the factoid, the executives, whose companies were very much like those on the list, were anxious and ready to hear what he had to say about solutions.

7. **Try an analogy:** use a comparison between two seemingly unrelated things. Great for explaining anything complicated or obscure. For instance: 'Our company without advertising would be like a lion with no roar.'

8. **Mention a topical or a current event:** something powerful and relevant from the day's news can be a great opener.

9. **Describe an imaginary situation:** if you do this it's best to be quite specific about what you want people to imagine rather than leave it too open. For example: 'Imagine it is 2005 and we have just been voted the most sought-after company by Forbes Magazine', rather than 'Imagine it is 2005 and we are a successful, growing company.'

## Middle

### *Signposts or Agendas*

Signposts are useful headings for the areas that you plan to cover. They need to be brief, usually one word, descriptions. Don't get wordy here or it gets very confusing for the listener. The general rule of thumb is to try not to have more than three or four areas to cover in any presentation and keep your signposts to broad areas you'll cover. Don't confuse your signposts with a lengthy table of contents – I've seen this so many times – and have ten or twenty items listed.

Your decision as to the order or sequence of your material is important. You need to tell your listener what order you're using and, if the order is important, why you've chosen that order.

For instance, you might list:

- Problem, options, solution
- Objective, strategy, steps to implement the strategy
- Idea, how it comes together, what it will cost
- Last year, this year, next year

The order will depend on the content but must be logical and easy to follow.

### Transitions

When you give a talk or presentation you need to take your listeners by the hand at the beginning and lead them gently to the end. Good transitions are the way to do this beautifully. A transition is what you say that tells people that you're moving between one section or signpost and the next. Good transitions are simple, relevant and clear, not stilted or obvious.

Here are some examples of general, easy-to-use transitions:

- With this in mind, I would like to. . .
- Let's begin . . . I would like to focus specifically on. . .
- Pause . . . I would like to recommend. . .
- Which brings me to. . .
- To start with. . .
- So, let's begin with the background. . .
- Let's look at x to begin with. . .
- Now, let's move on to. . .
- Next, we come to. . .

- Our next important area is. . .
- Finally, we have. . .
- Let's examine. . .
- So, let's pull all the elements together. . .

If you've been speaking for a long time in any section, it may be helpful to do a mini-summary of that section before moving on. This should be no more than a short sentence that re-focuses (nice word for wakes up) your listener.

You can use phrases such:

- So, that's a look at. . .
- As you can see, we have. . .
- That covers. . .
- In a nutshell, then. . .
- So, we've discovered that. . .
- Reviewing what we've discussed. . .
- So, the most important things to remember are. . .
- In summary. . .

## Ending

This is where you give your summary and conclusion. Closing your meeting or presentation properly is important. So often the presentation finishes with, 'OK, thanks for coming'. . . and that's it.

At the end of your presentation you need to give a brief summary of what you've talked about, restating key ideas, and to make your main point absolutely clear. This may be a conclusion, a request or a recommendation. The audience should know exactly what you think, believe or want and what you expect of them.

Be sure your conclusion is delivered with the right amount of energy and conviction. I say the right amount because I've heard too many advisers say it needs to be done with enthusiasm and dynamism. This may not always be the case.

Sometimes humility and respect or understatement is very powerful. Do the right thing for the situation.

As well as summarising your key conclusions you need to mention any follow-up. For example, where any meetings might be, what has to be done before another meeting and any next steps.

Then thank everyone for their time and attention and any contribution they may have made.

## CHOOSING YOUR STRUCTURE

Now you know the basics that apply to any structure, you can choose an appropriate structure for your particular situation. The more appropriate and relevant the structure the more successful you'll be.

### Short Structure One: Nice and Simple

This one is great for those times when you've been asked to say something on the spur of the moment, with no time to prepare. A lot of people panic when they're unexpectedly asked to say something. But there's no need – the following simple outline works every time. Of course you need content but if you keep this simple approach in mind it will help you immensely. It's called a Tell 'em outline. Tell 'em what you're going to tell 'em, tell 'em, then tell 'em what you've told 'em. The US army have claimed it as their own but it's also been attributed to Aristotle.

I like to call it the table-napkin outline – I have written impromptu talks on these wonderful bits of paper many times using this approach.

You can do this in your head once you get the hang of it, as you are walking to the front of the room or while you are being introduced. Perfect for weddings, funerals and anything in between!

## The Tell 'Em Outline

### Prepare

Tell people what you are going to talk about and why. Before you do this, decide what your point is – in one sentence in your mind. Then think quickly of only one or two areas or issues you will deal with to make that point.

### Deliver

Do it briefly – don't be tempted to talk too much and be sure to stick to your key areas. These little impromptus are best kept to three minutes. If only uncles all over the world knew this before they stood up at weddings.

### Make sure

Wrap up. Make your point – it is so much more interesting for the listener!

### Example:

Let's say you've been asked by an association you've just joined to take three minutes to say a little about yourself. You might say:

(*prepare*) Thanks, everyone Good to meet you. I'm pleased to be here tonight as the newest member.

Let me tell you how I came to be here. The circumstances revolve around two key features in my life: my family and my decision to change my job. (*takes fifteen seconds*)

(*deliver*) My daughter and my husband were reading the paper one day and they saw an article about . . . ! (*brief story taking perhaps one minute*)

All this was happening around the same time that I decided to change my job. I used to do X until . . . *(brief story taking perhaps one minute)*

*(make sure)* So, you can see, my being here makes a lot of sense and fits into a wonderful series of events – not least of which involves the support of my family and my decision to run my own business. That's it. Thanks, and I look forward to a successful affiliation with you. *(takes thirty seconds)*

It's that simple. Remember, if someone asks you to say something at the drop of a hat, it is best if you can include something about which you feel familiar. Don't try to be brilliant. If you talk about what you enjoy or know something about you'll come across as more natural and convincing.

## Short Structure Two: Brief Presentations

This structure is for brief presentations or talks of around five to fifteen minutes. You may have been asked to educate, inform or share information but no recommendation or proposal is being made.

### The Short Presentations Outline

### Prepare

State your subject clearly and concisely, usually in one sentence.

### Outline your Signposts

Don't say too much here. Remember, you are just giving the brief section headings.

### Deliver
Now, cover those areas in the body of your presentation, in the order that you promised, with clear transitions between each section.

### Make Sure
Towards the end of your presentation give a summary restating the key ideas or messages from the body of the presentation. Because this is a short presentation, make sure you're not repeating things you've just said. Be brief and don't introduce new information here; it just gets confusing if you do.

### Conclusion
What do you want people to do or think as a result of your presentation? What are the next steps?

### Example:
You're been asked to give a short talk about the benefits of fresh fruit and vegetables.

*(prepare)* Today I would like to talk about the virtues of fresh fruit and vegetables.

*(signposts)* First I'll talk about the most popular and nutritious fruit, then a little about vegetables and, finally, some delicious ways for you to enjoy eating them both.

*(deliver)* OK, let me begin with fruit – nature's treats . . . *(transition into first section)*
(now *deliver your information*)

As you can see, fruit provides a very high level of the vitamins we all need and does it with a touch of sweetness . . . *(transition out of first section)*

Now let's explore vegetables . . . *(transition into second section)*
*(now deliver your information)*

There you have it: more variety than you probably imagined! *(transition out of second section)*

Finally, let me show you some ways you can enjoy eating them . . .
*(transition into third section)*
*(now deliver your information)*

I hope you're all hungry by now and ready to prepare your own feast. *(end of final section)*

*(make sure)* So we've looked at fruits, vegetables and ways to enjoy them and I hope you've been inspired to take a new look at them as part of your diet. *(summary)*

*(conclusion)* Eat more fresh fruit and vegetables. Your efforts will pay off in the form of good health.
I've organised something for all of you. It is a great season for pears and squash; go get some and prepare them with these recipes here – I have copies for you to take home. *(next steps)*

This structure is a very useful and proven way to get your message across clearly and concisely. It contains the key components of any good solid message. You can use it as a basic structure for most types of presentation situations, long or short, formal or informal.

## Persuasive Structures

Being persuasive takes a bit of extra preparation and energy. After all, if you're asking someone to part with money, make a commitment or try something they haven't considered before then you need to tell them in the clearest terms why they might want to do this, backing up what you say with convincing argument or evidence.

Things are often compounded by the fact that most people don't like to ask or don't know how to ask directly or clearly for what they want. Instead they dance around the issue, burying it in a cumbersome structure and leaving their listeners confused and unclear. At the end of many presentations I've been left wondering what I was supposed to say yes or no to. The bottom line is that if you don't ask (and ask clearly), you don't get. So, let's have a look at how to ask.

## Persuasive Structure One: Ask Up Front

This is one of two structures designed to give a persuasive message.

In this one your recommendation is going to come right at the beginning.

### The Ask Up Front Outline

#### Prepare

Make administrative remarks if appropriate. Then creatively focus their attention in whatever way you may have chosen.

Then make your recommendation. Tell them what you're asking for.

Be sure to be direct and clear and don't be shy about it! Sometimes the situation calls for this kind of confidence. For instance; 'I'm here today to recommend that you proceed with full participation', or, 'I recommend that you invest the full amount of 500', or, 'I think you should say yes to x [or no]; here's why', or, 'I'm going to explain why I think x is a great idea.'

### Outline Your Signposts
Make sure these will indicate the evidence you need to support your recommendation or request.

### Deliver
Give the evidence or arguments that will persuade your audience.

### Make Sure
Summarise what you have said.

### Conclusion
Restate your recommendation clearly and with confidence. Let your listeners soak it in. This is what you want – say it like you mean it!

The risks of this approach revolve mostly around getting it wrong – what if your listeners are not ready to receive this kind of straightforwardness from you? They may not know enough about you or your recommendation to be comfortable with hearing it so early. Maybe you need to build credibility or educate them before you can do this. You need to judge this based on what you know.

### Choose this approach if

- They know what you want already (why waste time building up to it?)
- You want to come across as dynamic and confident
- It is your listener's preferred approach
- Your listener has a short attention span or is tired
- What you are asking is controversial or bold
- The listener knows you and trusts you
- You want to communicate a sense of urgency
- You're the last presenter at the end of the day and you don't want your listeners to have to work too hard

## Persuasive Structure Two: The Slow Reveal

This structure is the opposite of the previous one. In this case the request or recommendation is saved until the end of your presentation and your approach is indirect.

### The Slow Reveal Outline

### Prepare

After your administrative remarks and creative focus, move on to your subject. Don't say what you'll be asking for directly, introduce it as a sort of 'promise' of things to come. For instance: 'I'm going to be talking about the funding proposal. But before I go into detail, let me take you through . . .'

You can be a bit more tantalising than this if you wish to. For instance: 'I'll be talking about the funding proposal and I think you'll be excited about the changes we've made . . .'

### Outline Your Signposts

Now lead straight into your signposts, thinking of them as stepping stones to the request or recommendation you want to make.

### Deliver

The body of your presentation now reveals your recommendation bit by bit. A classic structure here is to identify the opportunity or the problem first, then explore alternatives before proposing a solution. This is where the listener finally hears what you want.

### Make Sure

At the end, be sure to summarise by restating the key points from the presentation.

## Conclusion

This is where you need to restate your recommendation absolutely clearly, so that the listener is in no doubt about what you want and this is what they take away from your talk.

This is a lower-risk approach, but may not work well if your audience is tired, impatient or already knows what you want.

### Choose this approach if

- The people you're speaking to like this approach and will give you the time to work through your idea
- Your listeners don't know enough about you or the idea for you to spill the beans yet
- Your listeners are the type of people who like to hear how you think and to understand the process before they will accept your idea
- You want to show off a little
- You need to learn a little more about them before you ask them for something specific
- You want to build suspense
- You want to keep the freedom to change the recommendation towards the end of your presentation, based on what you learn during the meeting
- Someone in your audience is hostile towards your idea and you need to build support first

## Other Useful Structures

There are a few other structures which can be useful in particular situations. Here are the ones that are most often used.

## Useful Structure One: Executive Summary

Sometimes you may be asked to send along a written report or outline ahead of your presentation. Whenever this happens there needs to be an executive summary, but I can't count the times that I have seen long-winded, boring, unimaginative executive summaries given as a response to a tender or proposal. The result is that few people have the time to wade through these documents before the meeting.

This is a shame because a good, crisp executive summary can set the scene perfectly before your presentation. So, make it a habit to give people the short, manageable version!

The most useful approach here is called: Situation, Complication, Resolution. It's a storytelling pattern that makes it instantly easier to put together an executive summary along with your presentation.

### The Situation, Complication, Resolution Outline

#### Situation
This is a brief description of the known situation. Keep it brief and to the point. No build-up.

#### Complication
This is a description of the thing or event that has 'destabilised' the situation. It will allow the listener to raise the question to which you will provide the response or resolution. For example, something that has changed or gone wrong or a future event that may affect the current situation.

#### Resolution
This is where you outline the question that is raised and the answer you give for it.

## Example

*(situation)* Over the past few years, our fundraising effort has been extremely successful. We were the only organisation focusing on this issue.

*(complication)* However, this year a newcomer has come on to the scene and our donors are confused by what appears to be two organisations doing the same thing.

*(resolution)* So, what are we going to do to deal with this new addition to the market? I believe we need to change our image and make a fresh approach to donors.

This approach is a clever way to set the tone of your response to a proposal. It will get your reader focused and interested in the details of what you are going to propose.

I find it works well to do the executive summary earlier in the planning and preparation rather than later. Sometimes if you do it earlier it can act as a compass – a navigational tool for the rest of the document.

Make it look different from the rest of the document. Imagine that it will be 'torn out' and passed around to initiate early decisions.

## Useful Structure Two: Building New Business

This is a great structure I have seen for initiating new business or presenting your 'credentials'. Imagine someone has asked you to come in and explain your idea or to compete with others for the business.

Your intention in this situation should be to make the listener feel they made the right decision by inviting you to the meeting. You want to help them imagine how it would be to work with you and to like the idea. This is how people who win are doing it:

### The Building New Business Outline

#### Here's what I know about you

This is where you demonstrate what you already know and understand about your listener's business and your willingness to learn more.

Most people talk first about themselves, so it's refreshing for someone to begin by talking knowledgeably about the person or business they are approaching. Make an effort to generate some ideas about the client's business and have some great questions to ask them. This is an opportunity for you to make your homework pay off and show some insight.

#### Here's what I can do for you

Here is where you show how you are best suited to meet or solve the listener's needs. Now is when you talk about which particular aspects of what you do could assist them, but only in the context of the listener and how they will benefit from your relationship. Use lots of evidence, case studies and examples.

#### Here's what it would be like to work together

This can be where you make it come to life by talking about other relevant aspects of you and your organisation that would be of benefit to them. Now can also be the time to go into the engine room and show how things would actually work if you were to get started. This is where you outline what you actually deliver and how we do it. It can include the nitty-gritty of fees, logistics etc.

### Useful Structure Three: The CEO Model

Most of my very experienced senior clients like this as their 'rule of thumb' approach to the request to do an impromptu appearance. It's a grown-up version of the 'Tell 'em' outline I described earlier.

### *The CEO Model*

### Focus their attention
Make a short dramatic point, maybe something funny, controversial, intriguing – something they may not expect. Make sure you draw the connection to the subject you are discussing.

### Relevance
Explain the relevance of your subject to the audience.

### Message
Make your key statement/recommendation.

### Evidence
Use two or three examples: illustrations, stories, anecdotes, case studies or points of personal relevance to support what you're saying.

### Summary
Restate two or three of your key benefits or points. No new information here.

### Conclusion
Relate your conclusion back to the main message.

## Useful Structure Four: Storytelling
It's hard to tell a story without rambling. This structure will help you tell stories that have a point instead of wandering around and becoming vague or over-long.

It will make it is easier to remember them – for you and the listener. It's called Event, Point, Relevance and it's most useful as a structure within a structure, that is, for when you wish to tell a story as part of another structure.

## *The Event, Point, Relevance Outline*

### Event
This is where you tell your story, briefly.

### Point
Now you come quickly to the point, the reason why you have chosen this particular story.

### Relevance
At this stage you tell the listener why this story is relevant to them or to the presentation or message you are giving.

### Example
I had a client who wanted to inspire her management team. She decided to tell the story of Ellen MacArthur's single-handed yacht race around the world. Her story is one of great courage and the ability to realise her goals and achieve a dream. A good story for motivating and encouraging others.

*(event)* A diminutive Englishwoman sails around the world. Some would say her finishing was against the odds. Particularly towards the end when she experienced critical breakdowns and nearly capsized.

*(point)* Most people thought she would quit.

*(relevance)* Big goals are never achieved without strong resolve and vision. Despite doubts and fears, press ahead and gain rewards.

## Useful Structure Five: Meetings
This structure is an outline of how a good meeting should go. Keep the following points in mind when you prepare for

a meeting: What is my purpose? What do I need to say to get my message across? What do I want people to do as a result of the meeting?

## Non-business conversation
This is the time for friendly, rapport-building conversation before the official part of the meeting begins. Put the focus on the other person or people, taking an interest in them.

## Ask questions
See if you can ask some good, relevant, prepared questions to gain a little more information about the other people so you can better tailor your message. This allows you to uncover real needs and learn something you might not have known.

## Rethink
After learning something from your probing, you may want to rethink your approach. Adjust a little here and there on the run.

## Present your message
This is where you put across the main issue or issues the meeting needs to address.

## Deal with objections
Often, after or during your presentation, you may get objections. Look on them as invitations that show the other person is listening and wants to know more. Deal with them calmly and in a friendly way.

## Close the meeting
Restate the agreements you have reached and some of the key things you need to do next.

## Follow-up

After the meeting make sure you fulfil your promises and do what you have said you'll do.

## Running a Meeting

If you're in charge of the meeting you want to make sure that it runs to plan, doesn't get out of control and that everyone's objectives are met. I've used the following technique over the years to help me plan and deliver meetings with much more ease. It allows you to run meetings effectively without over-controlling them.

Here's how it works:

- **Who:** make sure you have a list of who will be there, with names and roles. This is important when people may be coming together who don't know each other, or for when someone has special skills or contributions to make. No surprises
- **What:** make sure everyone knows what the meeting is trying to achieve. For example: 'Today, we're exploring the key issues to do with the launch of our idea in May. In order to do this, we will be looking at some recent research and opening the meeting to discussion on how each of us can contribute to the overall success of the launch.'
- **Why:** you need to outline the purpose and importance of the discussion. This could be brief or require further explanation. For example: 'We want the launch to be our most successful to date.'
- **How:** the agenda should describe how it will be done, including how people are to act (questions, no-judgements, time allowed for each person to speak, etc.) and the ground rules, timing, breaks, etc.
- **Outcome:** what do you want each person to leave with at the end of the meeting? For example: 'I'd like each of us to leave having agreed to do at least one thing to help the launch.'

## WORKING WITH STRUCTURE

There are, of course, more structures to choose from than I've outlined in this chapter. But the ones I've chosen are those you're most likely to need and that are effective in most situations. Use this chapter as a useful reference section and choose an appropriate structure for any situation, formal or informal, in which you are required to present yourself or your message or idea.

Choose the structure that is right for you and for the audience you expect to have. You may not always know what the people you will be talking to are like, but you can usually make a fair guess, based on the circumstances.

Structure is great for you because it helps you to stay focused on what you want to achieve from your message or presentation and it allows you to do this with the minimum of preparation and effort.

And for your listener structure is a gift. It allows them to find out who you are, what you want and why you want it, without having to work hard or solve puzzles. That way they can concentrate on what matters – saying yes to you!

# 7

# GOOD QUESTIONS

*The greatest compliment that was ever paid to me was when someone asked me what I thought, and attended to my answer*
**HENRY DAVID THOREAU**

This chapter focuses on one of the most important communication skills we have: asking good questions. The ability to ask well-timed, well-thought-out questions is critical for gaining insight, gathering information and creating understanding between you and another person.

You may think that when you set out to persuade someone of something it is they, not you, who will be asking the questions. This may be true, initially, but as the discussion progresses there will certainly be questions you need or want to ask of them. The right questions can not only be informative as you build a picture of what is possible, but will be a vital tool in building rapport and communicating successfully.

In this chapter I will explain what a good question is and how you can learn to make most of your questions good ones. I will also identify the most useful types of questions to ask in certain circumstances, explain how to avoid the most common mistakes we all make and outline the vital listening skills that are such an essential part of asking the right questions.

We are all familiar with asking questions. After all, we do it every day of our lives. But when we're in situations that make us tense or that are new, surprisingly often we either fail to ask the right question or ask the kinds of awkward or misplaced questions that hold us back. A wrong question can put the other person on the defensive, result in a close-down situation or lead to unnecessary or useless information.

On the other hand, when you ask a good question the results can be magical. I've heard people say, 'Gosh, I never really thought about my situation in that way before. Thanks. That really helped.' And they did most of the talking! When you can ask good questions it will help you to identify real needs and interests, sort out objections, establish a little more control and build a meaningful relationship with the other person.

When we communicate with another person a lot of what occurs between us involves both people's perceptions and impressions, some assumptions, some bluff and a sprinkling of exaggeration and emotion. It's often difficult, with all this in the way, to get to people's real needs and desires. The noise that is between us all most of the time can lead to people leaving a meeting or an encounter with very different ideas of what happened, or going off in directions that waste time and energy.

That's where asking the right questions comes in. This is a tool that not only furthers understanding, but which can be used to make sure that everyone present has the same information and is clear about where things are going next. Many of us are aware of the power of asking good questions but we don't always know how to go about doing it. There are moments when we'd love to ask the right question but we hesitate, unsure about whether a question is acceptable, or uncertain about what to ask.

People often ask questions only to confirm what they think they know. And while this is fine, it is limiting. Few people know how to use questions to venture into the unknown.

I've often heard people say that asking questions feels like an imposition, or, worse, an inquisition. They feel they are prying. If this is happening you're either asking the wrong questions or being over-cautious. A good question is neither an intrusion nor an imposition. It will simply move both people forward.

In my experience, most people miss out on opportunities to ask questions, not because it wasn't possible, but because they have a problem with asking. Either they weren't prepared enough to know what they could ask or they felt shy about pursuing something. 'I couldn't ask *that*,' or, 'No, I never asked,' are the two most common responses to missing vital information or unchecked assumptions. One of my favourite sayings when I'm working with clients comes from my friend Betsy. She says: 'If you don't ask, you won't get.' Most of us need to change our thinking about asking. We need to see questions as invitations we make to others.

Of course it's important to be aware of the sensitivities of cultural differences when considering what kinds of questions to ask. For example, Japan and the United States are at opposite ends of the information-gathering spectrum. The Japanese have quite complex and formal social hierarchies. Exchanging information and insight between virtual strangers is not clear-cut because it's not appropriate to simply ask when you want information. The Americans, on the other hand, are far less formal and if they like you they may well give you more information than you bargained for!

Asking good questions requires some generosity on your

part. For a start, you need to know what you need to know, then resist the temptation to rush to conclusions, judge or think you know what someone is going to say. Instead you need to be genuinely curious and to listen one hundred per cent to what is being said. We all know what it's like to realise that someone has stopped listening halfway through what we're saying. We feel put down and annoyed. The ability to listen fully is a vital part of asking good questions and I'll be exploring it in more depth later in the chapter.

We all know what it's like to get it wrong. We've all asked a question we didn't really want an answer to. And we've all asked that question we wish we'd never asked and then cringed as we heard the sound of a shovel in the dirt.

But while getting it wrong is all too common, getting it right is simpler than you think and very rewarding. All it takes is the willingness to learn, a bit of genuine curiosity and a few straightforward techniques.

## WHAT IS A GOOD QUESTION?

When a good question is asked, a genuine and worthwhile exchange takes place between two people. A good question will bring you closer to your listener and at the same time give you new information.

When you ask a good question both you and the other person know that you are listening. It creates mutual respect and a willingness to exchange valuable information. The picture will become clearer, you'll understand what the other person is thinking and what will influence their decisions. This in turn will help you towards the best solutions.

Asking questions is like dancing. Do it wrong and you'll tread on your partner's toes, cramp their style or embarrass them. Get it right and you move together so easily that the whole thing is a pleasure. Even though you're still leading it's so subtle that your partner is barely aware of it and is happy to follow.

## Good Questions

- Show you have prepared
- Are asked with genuine interest
- Get the real answer to what you have asked
- Help your listener gain insight into their situation
- Allow you to move towards the best possible outcome
- Are appropriate and never intrusive
- Build rapport and understanding

## THE MOST COMMON MISTAKES WE ALL MAKE

Here are the mistakes it's all too easy to make. The good news is that they're also easy to avoid once you know what they are:

- **Lack of preparation:** no plan or idea of where we want to go or why we are asking certain questions. Part of the forward planning for any kind of meeting should involve a list of possible questions we will want to ask. All too often people end up throwing in questions that aren't really useful and simply waste time
- **Nervousness:** trying too hard or going too fast. If you race towards the questions or throw them in too early then people feel irritated or unnerved. When you're nervous the first thing to do is slow down. Take a deep breath and think carefully before you start on the questions
- **Asking multiple questions in the same breath:** 'So, do you like the plan? Did you feel the timing will work OK? What do you think?' This is often another symptom of nervousness but simply sounds rude and impatient. The listener doesn't know where to start and you lose control

- **Interrogating:** asking questions in a demanding, quick-fire or bossy way – forcing yes/no answers – will get you nowhere. Your listener will clam up.
- **Asking questions and failing to listen to the answers:** this often happens when you're too focused on the next question. You've got it all ready but you don't listen to the answer to your previous question. This can lead you off in the wrong direction. Had you listened fully you might then have asked a different question.


## TYPES OF QUESTIONS

Although we all use questions every day we are rarely aware of the types of questions we're using. Getting to know these types is valuable because it gives you a choice. One type of question can be disastrous in a situation where another type of question might work well.

When you are using persuasive communication each type of question will have a role to play. Use the right questions at the right time and you will help your cause enormously.

### Closed Questions

These questions are wonderful if you want specific information or brief, pointed answers. But used in the wrong context they can shut down a conversation. A great example of this is the cocktail-party conversation with someone you don't know. You're shy, they're reserved and you're standing there trying to think of something interesting to say. So, you start on the questions:

- Do you come here often?
- What do you do?
- How long have you been doing that?
- Do you enjoy it?

The answers to these questions are likely to be one or two words long and the other person will soon feel they're under interrogation as you struggle to keep things going by asking more and more questions! All too soon you'll run out of things to talk about. Embarrassed pause. Cue to escape. Misery.

There is, however, a good time and place for closed questions. When time is short and you want to get down to specifics they're great.

They usually involve words and phrases such as: When? Where? How many? How much? How long? Who? What?

Closed questions are yes/no questions and either/or questions. 'Do you like football?' 'Do you want the pink one or the black one?' 'Do you want to go out for a meal?'

Closed questions can also be very useful for bringing things to a conclusion if someone is rambling for a little too long. 'So, do we all agree then?' can focus minds and bring results delightfully fast.

## Open Questions

Open questions are the polar opposite of closed questions. They invite long answers and are great to use if you want to explore thoughts, feelings and attitudes. Therapists love them.

The right time to use open questions, especially in a work context, is once a basic level of rapport has been established and at a point where more information would be really useful.

If you ask open questions in a friendly and interested way you are likely to get revealing answers, so if you're looking for more detail or inside information then this is the kind of question to ask.

But, like closed questions, open questions used on their own can create problems.

Take the cocktail-party scenario. A couple of open questions might get things going nicely.

- Could you tell me more about the work you do?
- I'd love to know what you think about politics
- How did you feel when you got divorced?

Trouble is, too many of these and you'll be there all night as the other person pours out their life story. And once again you'll be looking for a way to escape.

Open questions use phrases such as: What do you think about? What are your feelings about? Why? How? What methods? Would you give me an example of . . . ? Would you elaborate on . . . ? What is your opinion on . . . ? Tell me about.

Open questions can be very useful for getting the flow going if a meeting is feeling a bit stilted and awkward.

## Closed and Open Questions Combined

Closed and open questions are at opposite ends of the energetic spectrum. What they have in common is that if you use them exclusively you will end up in a mess. If you use only closed questions your conversation can end up rapidly dying. Use only open questions and you may end up wandering aimlessly around.

The best bet is to mix them up a bit. Use a few of each. Think of the two of them as punctuation. The open-ended questions are commas. The closed-ended ones are full stops.

For example:

- When did this project start? (*closed*)
- What were the ideas behind it? (*open*)
- Which aspects are key to your success over the next few months? (*closed*)
- Why is aspect x particularly important? (*open*)
- Do you think you will make your deadline? (*closed*)

The sensitive use of a combination of open and closed questions can work wonders, whatever your situation. Start to notice which kinds of questions you are using and experiment a little, so that you're more aware of the right moment for either sort of question. In particular, an open question can save the situation when a series of closed questions is in danger of shutting things down.

## Follow-up Questions

Sometimes you may want to encourage someone to give you a bit more information or to keep talking. This is where a follow-up question can be useful. They've given you a brief answer, now ask for more.

Use phrases such as: Could you tell me a bit more? Could you go into that in a bit more detail? I wonder if you could explain that? They'll open things up and get the information flowing. These are open follow-up questions and they're an invitation to give you more information.

You can use closed questions as follow-ups, too. If the person's answer goes on too long or rambles a bit, or things aren't getting to the point, you may need to ask a specific question.

'Have you got a deadline for the project completion?' is a closed question that can bring things neatly to a conclusion.

## Leading Questions

Leading questions can be really useful in the world of work when you're talking to an uninformed respondent or you want to help focus the answer in some way.

Leading questions are often portrayed as a bad thing because they include assumptions or information about the person being asked, and if this is negative, as in 'How often do you kick your dog?' then objections can be raised.

Courtroom dramas often include leading questions from

advocates and admonitions from judges for asking them. However, that scenario gives only one aspect of leading questions. For example: 'Do you think we should try the third option?' 'Do you believe construction works better when brick is used?' or, 'Do you agree that the third candidate was the best one for the job?'

The drawback is that a leading question may mean that the listener won't really think for themselves. They may agree because they think it's what you want to hear. But then you may be fine with this.

## Take-a-guess Questions

If you want someone to speculate, hypothesise or guess – ask them to. You can get a lot of information and insight by asking the other person to make a prediction.

Try questions such as 'What do you think is actually going to happen?' 'What do you think the result will be?' 'What's your estimate of how long it will take?' or, 'What kind of funding do you expect to get?'

If the person you're asking is willing to go along with you and take a guess it may prove very useful – as long as you remember that it's a guess.

## Hypothetical Questions

This type of question can help the other person take a position based on hypothetical assumptions or situations. It can help you both think more creatively.

For example: 'If I could find a way to reduce the amount of time you would need to spend on the project, would you consider being an advisor?' 'If we were to relocate would you come with us?' or, 'If you lost your job tomorrow what would you do?'

Hypothetical questions ask the listener to take a leap into

the unknown but can be extremely productive and open up positive discussion.

## Either/Or Questions

This is a type of closed question that I've referred to before and which can be very useful in specific situations.

Perhaps you want them to make a choice between alternatives. You want to check if the alternatives are right or maybe you need to narrow the discussion down. For example: 'If you do decide to go ahead, will it be in May or July?' 'Would you rather we increased the budget or worked with what's on the table?' or 'Shall we buy the shop next door or keep the business small?'

These questions can open discussion and can help you to see what the other person wants and thinks about a particular subject.

They're also useful for helping someone make a decision if they are waffling a bit.

## Reflective Questions

Reflective questions are used to indicate that you understand what is being said by the other person. They're a way of double-checking and at the same time of indicating that you've got the message.

They're also useful for summing up a very long statement or a series of complicated statements from the other person by reflecting back their key points. For example: 'Let me ensure that I understand: from what you have said, you need to secure the commitment of the consular office first, but you will continue to push the campaign through in the hope that you will get a yes?' or, 'Tell me if I've got this right: you want to commission me, but you need agreement from the director before you say yes?'

### Find out the Priorities

This question can help you establish priorities during a discussion. It's a good way of being clear about where the other person's goals and priorities lie.

For example, you might say: 'Of all the issues we have discussed (timing, who's involved, cost, conflicts), which will be the most problematic?' or, 'Is this the most important area as far as you're concerned?' or, 'Which area would you deal with first?'

### Work out the Criteria

I like this one because it is so uncomplicated and often clarifies what you think you know about how a decision will be made. For example: 'What criteria will you use to make the decision?' or, 'What do you need to know before you go ahead?' It often also helps the person articulate exactly how they will make the decision and any barriers or objections that may exist become clearer.

## LISTENING WHILE ASKING

Listening is hugely important and often underrated. A group of people together often spend the whole time fighting to get their own word in, and rarely are they truly listening to what any of the others has to say.

Listening is probably the most important ingredient of asking good questions. If you haven't listened to the answer someone gives to what you have asked, then how can you respond with a good question?

Most of us are guilty of interrupting people while they speak. We either cut them off, 'yup-yup' through their comments, finish their sentences for them, look away or start to fidget. Usually we're thinking about what we're going to say before they're finished and so we hardly hear them.

These bad habits can be cured. The more aware of them you are the easier it is to stop.

Follow these guidelines to dramatically improve your listening skills. The better you are able to listen the easier it will be to establish rapport and to gather the information you want.

## Acknowledge

We've all met the annoying person who grunts or exclaims through our conversation to the point of distraction. Doing this is rude and usually a sign that the person isn't really listening.

However, there are small noises or gestures you can make to politely coax or invite the other person to continue. Small grunts, 'hmm's, 'aha's, 'oh's, nodding slightly up and down or a very soft-spoken word or phrase, such as 'Really' or 'I didn't realise that' can all encourage.

You can also use small acknowledgements to let the person know that you have understood and invite them to go on. For example: 'I understand what you mean', 'Interesting' or 'I'm with you'. They are fairly non-committal but have a positive impact on the flow of the conversation.

## Validate

If the person you are talking to contributes an idea or an alternative that you like, don't be afraid to compliment them. People often withhold compliments through embarrassment, stinginess or thoughtlessness.

Validating what someone has said makes them feel good while affirming that you have heard and understood what they are saying. For instance: 'That's a really good idea, Sarah. I hadn't thought of that', 'What a good suggestion', or 'I like that. Thanks.'

## Share

This means that as you talk you offer a little bit of your own experience or viewpoint. For instance: 'I feel the same way about that' or 'That's been my experience, too.'

Sharing like this is a means of empathising with the other person and creating a connection that will strengthen your rapport.

Be careful, though: don't monopolise the conversation and shift the focus to yourself with a long story about what happened to you or how you went through just the same kind of trauma. Keep it short and simple. Even if you see lots of things to share, don't keep butting in to share each one. Piling up things you share doesn't necessarily make you more interesting.

## Pausing

When we ask a question and the answer isn't given immediately we can often find the silent gap uncomfortable and leap in by answering our own question, or asking another.

This can be a mistake. It may be that the person simply needs time to think and we can miss vital information by cutting them off. Besides which, it's rude. Wonderful things come if you wait after you ask a question. Keep the intention friendly – you're not trying to make the other person uncomfortable, just letting them have the space to find the answer.

You can also pause after they have answered the question, because they may add more. This pause can be unnerving if you haven't signalled that you've heard the answer, so be sure to add a brief acknowledgement after they respond. Don't be tempted to add to it – let it happen and you may be surprised.

## Ask one question at a time

Try hard to avoid multiple questions. If you ask two, three or four questions in one, as in 'What do you think of the latest amendments to the contract, do you agree with them, do you think they'll cause trouble among the members, what do you think they'll do?' you'll confuse your listener. Then you'll tend to get partial or disjointed answers. The other person won't be able to remember all the questions and will probably answer just one of them, if any.

Asking multiple questions is a sloppy habit that usually stems from nerves and bad planning. Take a deep breath, slow down and ask one at a time. It also helps to rehearse your questions if you have a tendency to ask too many at once.

## Summarise

Most of us understand the importance of summarising at times during a conversation to ensure we understand. This can be particularly important at the end of the conversation to clear up any points or restate certain things for emphasis. Summing up is important because it signals 'completion' of parts of your meeting/conversation and allows for a smoother moving on. The other person will know that you have heard and understood what has been said or agreed.

For instance: 'So, I think we have discussed all the issues around the launch date. If you agree, why don't we move on to the next step?'

## PLANNING YOUR QUESTIONS

Before any kind of important meeting or exchange take a little time to plan your questions. Most people plan what they want to say but forget the questions that might follow, assuming that questions will just arise naturally from whatever is said. Not true. Doing it that way often means that important information is missed.

Here's a straightforward guide to planning your questions:

## Earn the Right to Ask Questions

You won't be popular if you weigh in with dozens of questions right at the beginning. It's better to earn the right to ask them first. How? By preparing carefully for the meeting and planning your questions ahead of time. Then by waiting patiently until the right point in the meeting to begin asking questions. This will be once the main information has been exchanged and you and the other person have an idea of one another's positions. This may be early on in the meeting – for instance, if you need some clarification before you go on – or later. The important thing is to be flexible and choose the appropriate moment. The questions you plan before the meeting will be a useful guide and will focus your thinking both before and during the meeting, even if you don't ask them all exactly as planned.

Earning the right to ask also means being sensitive and treating the other person with respect. No diving in with awkward questions in the hope that this may kick-start something.

## Plan the Timing of Your Questions

You can't ask some things early on. Be aware of what you might ask at each stage of a meeting. Earlier questions may be more formal and general. Detailed or more personal questions may come later, when you get the clear impression that it's OK to ask.

## Have a Purpose in Mind for Each Question

Sometimes people get carried away with friendly 'going

nowhere' questions that are nice – for a while. Then it gets annoying. You end up talking about things that aren't relevant or important.

So, ask questions that are going to lead you both down the path that you want to be on. If you find yourself straying, then bring the conversation right back to the point.

### Practise the Questions You Want to Ask with a Friend

Make sure your questions are clear, relevant and not intrusive by practising them on a friend who will role-play the other person in the meeting.

This gives you a great opportunity to hear what they sound like out loud and to alter anything that is jarring and add anything that is missing. Your friend might say, 'But you didn't ask me about x,' and you'll realise you've missed something very obvious.

### Ask Questions That Matter

By this I mean ask the questions that get you to the information you genuinely want to know about the other person.

I was on a date once where the man I was with exhausted me with four hours of interrogation. By the end of the evening I felt tired and annoyed and he hadn't learned anything of importance about me because his 'magazine-style' questions – 'What do you hate?' 'What do you love?' 'Give me three words that describe you' – got shorter and shorter answers. Besides which, he never let me finish anyway!

This man was looking for information, and got very little. But what he had no clue about was insight. Your questions need to look for insight about the situation or person, not simply information. And to gain insight you must ask questions carefully, thoughtfully and with awareness.

## Be careful you don't pry

You're prying when you go too far in your questioning, accidentally or not. Perhaps you've been asked to stay away from a certain subject, or to stop at a certain point. If you push it you're likely to put backs up and get doors slammed. Good manners count for a lot.

## Here's your at-a-glance question planner

- Decide which areas or issues need to be asked about
- Sort out the order, what you need to ask about first, second and third
- Choose and design specific questions for each of these areas
- Decide whether any of the areas you want to ask about need you to set up or introduce before you start asking questions
- Bring the questions you've planned to the meeting with you, but be prepared to be flexible

## THE INSTANT RESCUE PLAN

There are times, for all of us, when things go wrong. When no matter how carefully you've prepared, you make a great big mistake. Or you see the look of horror/irritation/boredom on the other person's face and realise your line of questioning leaves a little to be desired.

In those moments when you wish the ground would swallow you up, or at the very least that the meeting would draw to a rapid end and you could crawl away somewhere very dark, don't despair. There's always something you can do to change track and begin to put the situation right.

Here are some of the problems you might encounter:

- You hit resistance to a specific area of questioning. If this is happening then don't keep going back there. Don't push when someone clearly doesn't want to answer. Find another way around. Your answer might arrive via another area of discussion

- The other person doesn't seem to understand your question. Make sure your question is clear. If need be, rephrase it more simply

- You don't seem to be getting anywhere. The meeting is going on and you don't feel as though you're making any real progress. When this happens bring the discussion to a head with a question such as: 'So, what are you thinking?' It can work like a dream

- Your listener seems agitated. Chances are that you're prying, whether you meant to or not. Or perhaps you've just touched on what is a sensitive area for this person. Sometimes the best way to soothe things is to bypass the question and summarise the agreements you have reached so far or the key points and ask if you're on track. This will take the focus off how the other person is feeling and move it into a safe area

## WHEN IT'S RIGHT

It's worth putting time and effort into asking good questions. The people you ask will appreciate you for it, you'll learn what you need to know and everyone will leave feeling good.

By developing our listening skills – and only practice can really turn you into a good listener – you'll discover how to keep your questions relevant and appropriate.

By using the right questioning technique at the right time, never rushing and giving the other person plenty of time to reply, your questioning skills will become an art form, a valuable tool in your toolbox of skills.

A good question can rescue a bad situation, create rapport, introduce humour to defuse tension, discover hidden information and impress others with your insight and understanding. So, use one!

# 8

# COLD CALLING

*Well, if I called the wrong number why*
*did you answer the phone?*
**JAMES THURBER**

It sounds so simple. Just pick up the phone, call someone you don't know and ask for something you want. Easy, right?

Or perhaps not. Most people hate cold calling so much that they'd rather climb Everest with a toothpick than have to do it. Some of the world's largest and most successful companies have a real problem getting their most experienced and highly paid people to do it. Fear of cold calling is so common that entire businesses have popped up just to help people overcome it.

There are an awful lot of people coming up with something else to do rather than pick up the phone. For them it's in the 'don't-touch-that' bucket along with the fish guts and the cigarette butts.

Why does this simple act inspire such dread and horror? People describe cold calling as being cast out to sea, or in the dark. They feel it's undignified, humiliating and associated with being desperate.

I smile as I write this, not out of disrespect for the millions who feel this way but because of how simple and unscary it can be. With a relatively easy turn of the knob on one's attitude dial and a few skills, cold calling can become easy to do, hugely productive and, dare I say it, even fun.

This chapter will dispel the myths about cold calling, help you pick up the phone more easily and show you how, with a bit of mental and practical preparation, you can turn the cold-calling nightmare into a success story.

## WHY WE HATE COLD CALLING

Here are the top reasons clients have given me for hating cold calling:

1. I hate rejection.
2. I hate rejection.
3. I hate rejection.
4. People don't want to be bothered by me.
5. I hate selling on the phone.
6. I don't have enough experience to do it well.
7  I can't do it unless I know what to say.
8  So-and-so is too busy.
9. I'll never get past the assistant – he/she is too controlling.
10. This kind of thing is just not me.

Recognise these? You can probably come up with a whole lot more. What they all have in common is a lack of confidence and a belief in failure. You expect it to go wrong, put yourself in the 'I'm not worthy' position and surprise, surprise, it goes badly.

Yet all it takes to turn things around is a shift in attitude and some careful preparation.

## HOW TO MAKE (AND ENJOY) COLD CALLS

Here's my ten-step, foolproof plan for changing the way you see cold calls and making them as easy as chatting to a friend.

### 1. Start Making Warm Calls

Guess what? There's no reason why you should ever have to make a cold call again. Great news, isn't it?

'Cold' implies miserable, unpleasant and that you are starting from zero, with no knowledge of the person you are calling or how to make a connection with them.

It implies that you think what you have to say will mean nothing to the other person.

So, let's forget about cold calls. From now on you only make warm calls.

Warm calls are about making good connections between people who can benefit one another. Warm calls are friendly, easy and fun. Warm calls are productive, effective and positive.

'Go out and make a friend' is a wonderful thing a colleague said to me once. Nice way to think about it.

### 2. Get Your Attitude Right

Don't approach a cold call believing that the other person has all the power. You're calling because you've got something to offer, an idea, opportunity or service. The person on the other end may want what you have to offer; they certainly deserve to hear about it.

The only genuine barrier to a successful cold call is the attitude we bring to it. Making a cold call with the wrong attitude is asking for failure. When we dread it we invite it to go wrong.

Let me explain. You need to make a cold call. You're sitting by the phone. You wonder if you will be bothering this person by calling. You think that perhaps you should send a letter first because a call is a bit brash. You imagine the person won't have any interest and will reject you. You're afraid that calling too soon may look desperate – but leaving it too long may look like you don't care. You're afraid of seeming pushy.

Thoughts like these will paralyse you. When or if you do finally make the call you'll probably sound awful. Being timid, cautious, apologetic or pathetically grateful will simply put the other person off.

What's more, you have no idea whether any of these miserable thoughts is true. The likelihood is that none of them is true. How do you know how the other person feels?

To get over this kind of misery-inducing attack of fear you need to get your attitude right. Start believing that it's going to go well, that you'll build rapport with the other person, enjoy the call and end it with a successful result.

Remember that you have a lot to offer, you're warm, friendly and interesting and talking to you may be one of the high points of the other person's day. Think confidence and you'll sound confident. Sound confident and you're more than halfway there.

## 3. Be Prepared

The best way to make a successful cold call is to be prepared. Before you even pick up the phone, be sure you have a clear, concise answer to the question, 'What do you want?'

Put some time into planning your call. Prepare clear, brief explanations of who you are and what you would like.

Always keep your goal in mind. In most cases this is to get a meeting with the person you're calling. Take things one step at a time. Do the right amount of preparation for the call, concentrating on what you will need to say in order to achieve your goal. Don't jump three steps ahead and worry about the meeting. Once you've arranged it you can prepare for that.

## 4. Remember There are No Gatekeepers, Just Team Members

The person you have to talk to first, usually a secretary or assistant, is often known as the 'gatekeeper'. They hold the power to put you through – or not – to the person you really want to talk to.

I think the word 'gatekeeper' is unhelpful and negative. So let's forget about gatekeepers and think of them as team members instead. Don't think of this person as someone to get 'past' but a peer to the person you are trying to contact. Treat them that way. You need them on your side – as part of the team. Some people's secretaries and assistants are hired to protect them from the barrage of calls they get every day, so that they can get on with their jobs. Understandably you are going to have to work at getting to them.

The assistants are really important to you. You need them and must respect them. The main reason why most people don't get through is because the assistants can smell insincerity and don't like to be treated badly. You need to make it easy and desirable for them to pass you on because they often control the information flow between you and the person you want to see. You need them on your side.

I've found the following things useful to keep in mind when talking to assistants:

- Be polite. Be respectful – and introduce yourself
- Sound and *be* confident and cheerful
- Don't say too much. Keep your tone light and undemanding
- Don't get them too involved in the idea; you don't want them to feel obliged or in a situation where they have to 'sell' to or convince the person you want to see. That's your job
- Ask for their help if you need it. Maybe you need a better

strategy – such as a better time to call. Maybe you need to know a little more about the person or the organisation in general
- Think of them as friends. I have been blessed by 'gatekeepers' – or, as I prefer to call them, 'sentinels' – who have been wonderfully supportive towards me on many occasions. Thank you to them!

## 5. Be Ready for Anything

Sometimes VIPs pick up their own phone. Many years ago I called the office of a high-profile, 'impossible-to-reach' person. I was mentally and physically prepared to speak only to his secretary when, you guessed it, he picked up the phone. Needless to say, I didn't do well. I'm sure he could hear the surprise and a hint of panic in my voice. I fumbled through what I wanted to talk to him about and was kindly passed on to his assistant. Never to return again!

If you do want to reach the high-profile person direct then try calling their offices after hours or very early in the morning. And be ready!

Another time I was put through to someone I had been trying to reach for a couple of weeks. When I got through, we had a nice chat about why I was calling. He liked what he heard enough to include me in a conference call that was to take place in a few minutes time. I went from speaking to him to speaking to four of his colleagues based in four different countries. Each had an interest in what I offered but they had completely different needs. It was a situation in which I had to think on my feet. Rather than try to sell my service I concentrated on telling them enough to get them to want to meet and talk further, which worked well.

So, be ready to adapt, to be thrown in at the deep end or to go for it!

## 6. Use Links

The reality is, you probably know more about the people you want to meet than you think you do. Since you have decided to contact them there must be a common link, even if it is simply that they could benefit from what you have to offer.

A link, however distant, can also be a great point of introduction or ice-breaker. Rather than feel you barely know this person, use your common link as a jumping-off point.

It's a good enough reason to pick up the phone if you:

- Have already met them, at a conference, cocktail party or airport
- Have been referred to them by someone you both know
- Have written a letter introducing yourself
- Are a member of the same group or association
- Share an interest or hobby
- Have kids who go to the same school
- Are interested in information or knowledge that they have
- Read something they wrote – book, newspaper article, newsletter
- Were present at an event they also attended, even if you didn't meet
- Read something written about them such as an announcement of promotion, award, achievement

You may well come across other links that can work just as well. Any link is enough to get you rolling; use it and go from there.

## 7. Sound Interesting

A lot of people blow a cold call because they don't really sound interesting enough on the phone. They don't make their proposition enticing enough by using 'evidence' as they speak; they just dump information down the phone. It's almost as though they're talking to themselves. 'Look at how well I've memorised my stuff!'

You need to create a situation in which the other person wants to hear more. Don't just tell them everything you think they should know or give them a list of what you want. Remember, you're building rapport so that you can get face to face.

To get the other person really interested you must sound interesting. Introduce yourself clearly, keep your facts simple and then let the other person know what will be of value or interest to them.

Many people use a script as a kind of security blanket. I've always been against using word-for-word scripts because even the best of us don't sound natural or interesting when we're focusing on a script. Use notes as a reminder of some of the key information you want to say, but forget a verbatim script. Stay flexible. Don't be too insistent or speak so quickly that it sounds as if you're trying to get your words in before they hang up on you. They'll probably feel that meeting you will be a chore.

What you need to do is to seduce your listener. Not literally, of course, but the idea is to make them feel interested in what you have to say and in meeting you. I knew a woman who really used to 'seduce' her male clients into meetings. She would make her voice really low and sexy and laugh suggestively. She got plenty of meetings – and a few dates – but the problem was that she was pretty hopeless at following through with her business objectives.

### 8. Use Body Language

Research shows us that what most influences other people's impressions of us is our body language – the way we move and gesture. So, when the visual is removed – on the phone – your voice and tone take on a whole new level of importance.

However, you still need to consider your body language in order to make a positive impression with your voice over the phone. Your voice will reflect your level of energy, your attitude and how you are feeling and these will depend, to a large extent, on your posture.

When you're preparing to warm call, be sure you're physically comfortable – but not too comfortable. Your mind can't go where your body isn't, so if you lie on the sofa you may well sound as though that's what you're doing! Some people feel they have a higher level of energy when they're standing. Some like to sit in a businesslike, upright position and I've heard of others who like to put a mirror in front of them to create a more personal feeling. However you do it, be sure you feel positive, energetic and confident.

I've come across many examples of how posture can affect a person's phone voice. A client of mine was told that he mumbled into the phone. One look at him and I could see why: he sat so hunched over that his face was nearly on his desk and his hands were practically covering the receiver. Not surprising, as he was in an open-plan office and it was very noisy, but not great for his clients. Another client had a very long cord for his phone and used to pace around, which meant that his voice was very fast and slightly too loud. Another used a headset in order to leave her hands free while speaking to clients. Useful, but of course she does things with her hands and you could hear that she was not quite listening.

## 9. Don't Take it Personally

This one's very important because it's the guaranteed way to avoid feeling rejected. Rejection is about feeling that you, personally are wrong or not wanted. Let go of that idea and you can see the whole thing much more clearly. There are all kinds of reasons why people say no and rarely are they about you.

Just because someone doesn't take your call immediately doesn't mean they don't want to talk to you. Statistics show that most people who call to get meetings give up after two attempts. Make your skin a little thicker and hang in there for the third and fourth.

If you hear no – perhaps you're speaking to the wrong person. Check this. If your idea or approach is turned down then take another look at it and see whether there's anything you need to change or improve.

Finally, remember that some people will say no because they're having a bad day, feeling stressed or dealing with a problem. Don't feel you failed; accept that you didn't get there this time and be prepared to move on or try again.

## 10. Have Fun

Finally, I want you to think of using the phone as fun. Think of all the exciting possibilities that open up when you pick up the phone and call someone you don't know. Think of what you might be missing when you refuse to make that call. There are opportunities out there just waiting for you . to pluck up the courage and go for it.

A friend of mine met her husband through a cold call. He worked for a company she had to call when she was setting up her freelance catering business. She agonised over the call for three days, but she'll be glad she made it for the rest of her life.

The telephone is a communication tool, a means for you and the person at the other end to connect. Don't think of your call as intrusive. After all, the person at the other end is choosing to pick up the phone and is probably quite happy to talk to you. Most people don't mind taking a call if you are genuine and are sensitive to their time constraints. So, call them and have fun!

## MAKING THE CALL

Now that you have a different approach, you're almost ready to pick up the phone. But before you do go through this brief checklist:

### Before you pick up the phone

- Be sure you are comfortable – standing or seated
- Try saying the first sentence or two of what you plan to say over the phone out loud to yourself, in the tone you intend to use. This is good for warming up your voice and relaxing you
- Make sure you know who you want to contact and how to pronounce their name
- Be ready to answer the question, 'How can I help you?' with confidence and clarity
- Have in front of you key reminder points and any information you may need to refer to

OK, you're ready to make the call!

### After you pick up the phone

You have three to five seconds until the person at the other end of the line makes their first decision about you: do they want to carry on listening or try to get rid of you? This decision will be based largely on your tone of voice. Keep it natural, conversational, familiar but not over-familiar.

Keep in mind that your time and your listener's time is of equal value. Don't sound overly grateful or humble.

Use these three to five seconds is to introduce yourself and check whether it's a good time to speak. You may also have to explain why you are calling. Keep it short.

It is always good to say that you want to be brief – you tend to get a bit more time if you ask for a little.

### *Here are a couple of options*

'Hello. Is that John? John, my name is Jane Roper – we met at the eco conference last week. Is this a good time to talk?'

Or:

'Hello. John, my name is Jane Roper. I'm calling because I read that article you wrote in the *Chronicle* and wanted to ask you a few questions. Is this a good time for that?'

If you make it to the next step, give your reason for calling – in a few words. Make sure that your reason shows some understanding of them or their business.

Your listener is creating a picture of you through your voice and what you say. So, now is the time to say something meaningful and relevant. For instance, you can mention the name of someone you both know, mention a topical issue affecting them or something directly related to your idea.

Be prepared to answer the question, 'What's this about?' without going into too much detail about why you want to meet.

### *Try these options*

'I'd like to arrange a meeting with you to discuss the green-space project you're involved in. I know you spend a lot of time on this and it would be good to . . .'

Or:

'I hear you're on the board of directors and that you're concerned about x. I would like to meet and discuss a few proposals we have to expand x.'

Remember that a short answer creates the desire to hear more. You now have their attention and need to make the most of it.

I like to sum up what you need to get across to the other person with a simple formula: What + Why + Prove:

- What's in it for me?

- Why should I be interested?
- Prove it!

You've got a few minutes at most to answer these questions for the other person. So involve them. You can do this by referring to a need that your idea will address. Because you've prepared well and know a little about them, you're likely to be able to give a good reason (benefit) for meeting.

Keep your statements short and sweet and you'll make them 'juicier' and more interesting.

Here's what it might look like:

'John, I'm interested in talking to you specifically about some consulting work regarding protection from Rule 451 that I am doing with other greenspace companies.'

'Oh. OK. I don't have a lot of time. What exactly do you want?'

'I know that your recycling business is going to be subject to some changes under Rule 451 due out in September. I work with other greenspace companies X, Y and Z and have helped them minimise the costs associated with it. I'd like to meet you to see what I can do to help you.'

In this brief conversation Jane has told John what's in it for him and why he should be interested. She's added the proof by telling him that she's already helped other companies.

At the very least it will have him interested and they can talk a little more. Jane can now match her tone to John's. If he wants to chat further, then fine. If he is rushed and wants to end the call soon she can suggest they arrange to meet and leave it at that.

### After you put the phone down

Follow up with a note after your call, whether you arranged a meeting or not. Keep your letter or e-mail simple. Thank the other person for the call and remind them of the key points, agreements or next steps that resulted from the conversation. Do it right away so that the energy and tone of your conversation is still there.

Here's how it might look:

*Dear X,*
*It was a pleasure speaking with you today. Your project sounds exciting and full of promise.*

*As we discussed, I will be contacting you again on Wednesday of next week to follow up with Margaret. You mentioned that by then we should know the outcome of the board meeting.*

If you got a no over the phone you can still follow up with a brief, non-pushy note to say that you will try them again at a later date. People can and do change their minds.

Finally, make sure you do what you've said you will do.

## GET CALLING!

I hope that by now you're feeling better about the idea of making calls to people you don't know.

With the right information, preparation and attitude, making these calls can be fun and rewarding. And remember that the more you do it the easier it will become. Get in some practice by making calls to gather information and do research. Most people you talk to will be happy to help and will respond to your tone and style. Always sound conversational, respectful and interesting and you'll soon find that this kind of call holds no more fear for you than calling a friend.

# 9

# STICKY SITUATIONS

*It is not whether you win or lose but
how you play the game*

**ETON SCHOOL SONG**

The sticky-situation club is probably the one with more members than any other club on earth. Every one of us has had our fair share of sticky situations – and lived to tell the tale.

What are sticky situations? Well, remember those moments that make you go hot, cold and red-faced every time you recall the details? That's them. Sticky situations are the ones we'd rather not face, thanks very much, but somehow just can't avoid in life.

In my working life I've witnessed calm, sane and intelligent people transform into pink-faced, jittery, teary, confused blobs when they've been faced with these situations. And I've had quite a few blob moments myself, I promise you. Having the wind taken out of your sails with an abrupt criticism, an odd piece of behaviour, an aggressive comment or a moment of hideous embarrassment is tough. Not easy to keep smiling and recover. Mostly we want to run and hide. This chapter is about the kinds of sticky situations that crop up at the most important times of all, in situations when you want to give the best impression possible and come away glowing with success.

An unexpected sticky moment, and let's face it they're always unexpected, can be hard to recover from. There you are stammering, blushing, fumbling for answers and wishing a very big hole would open beneath you, just when you wanted to appear cool, calm, informed and in control.

Sticky situations can be salvaged, though. It is possible to recover from the stickiest and most uncomfortable moments, if you know what to do. But your intention in coping with a sticky situation is not to run and hide or to outsmart someone else, it is to maintain rapport.

A lot of sticky situations can be avoided in the first place with careful preparation. These are the ones that result from lack of information, little oversights or mistakes in the presentation. You can anticipate some of the most likely ones and be ready. But others will just come along, because upsets, surprises, difficult people and the unexpected are unavoidable. So, being prepared to respond in the best way possible and come through with a minimum of embarrassment and fuss will give you a huge advantage.

That's what this chapter is all about – facing those 'ouch' moments when you wish you hadn't got out of bed that morning and coming through them still primed for success.

When nothing throws you for more than a moment, when you can take a potentially awful situation and turn it around, then you know you've mastered the art of dealing with sticky situations.

They come in all shapes and sizes. A client I worked with was totally floored in the middle of a presentation when the man he was presenting to fell asleep. No amount of throat-clearing and tapping on the table could wake him. Nothing to do, short of giving him a vigorous shake, but wait for him to wake up. Which he did, half an hour later, at which point the presentation continued smoothly without a hint that there had been an interruption.

Then there was the friend of mine who'd spent weeks organising the opening night of her restaurant. When the day came the place looked perfect, the food was mouth-watering and lots of people turned up. Great – until the power failed for an hour and by the time the lights came on the food was cold and the critics had gone home. It turned out that my friend had allowed an acquaintance, who wasn't properly qualified, to do the rewiring in the building. Not a good move.

I've been in plenty of sticky situations myself. I remember once entering a room for a pitch only to discover that my potential client had asked a team competing against me to sit in on my presentation. I was taken totally by surprise but decided my best option was to use it as an opportunity to make the competition nervous and to learn more about them.

Why do sticky situations happen? Well some are simply accidents. But the rest fall into three categories. Those that are real and fair objections, those that are odd or mean things people do and those, like my friend's, that are your own little nightmares – the result of your own mistakes or bad preparation.

In the course of this chapter I'll go through some common examples of all three, with tips on how to deal with them. But first I want to give you the three vital strategies you need to cope with just about any sticky situation and come up smiling.

## STICKY-SITUATION STRATEGIES

In the event of a sticky-situation emergency take a hammer and break glass to release the following stick-proof solutions:

## Step 1: Re-establish Rapport

Make sure you're not thrown by what happened and keep your calm. Match the other person in tone, volume and pace so that they feel you've heard and understood them. And be sure to acknowledge the other person by saying something like, 'I can see you're upset by this', or, 'Thanks for your comment.'

Meanwhile, keep your sense of humour. It's your most important ally in a lot of sticky situations, so bring it out, dust it off, tickle it and send it to the gym. This doesn't mean laughing out loud or cracking jokes when things go wrong; in fact, trying to be funny in a sticky situation can often backfire because others may consider it rude or inappropriate. Keeping your sense of humour is a way of keeping things in perspective and remembering that most things aren't really that sticky and can be sorted out. If you have a sense of humour then when things go wrong it will never seem that bad.

A client of mine went into a meeting with a potential sponsor for her charity, wearing her smartest suit. Ten minutes later she knocked her cup of tea all over it. Warm, wet and very embarrassed, she had to continue. She wanted to cry, but instead she treated it as a minor mishap, laughed it off and went on to give the best presentation she'd ever done. And got the sponsorship.

If you refuse to take whatever has happened personally, even if it's a remark or insult aimed directly at you, then you win every time. Stay cool, unflustered and focused. Remind yourself that it says far more about the person who made the remark than you.

When you take things personally and allow yourself to feel hurt or angry, you get defensive. This takes you off your track and it makes it almost impossible to try to shift your attention back to the matter in hand. So, instead, take a deep breath, remember it's not about you and carry on.

Janie, a client of mine, told me about a time when she was in a meeting with a potential client who seemed edgy, nervous, bored and short-tempered. Several times during the meeting he left the room to take phone calls and at the end he cut the meeting short very abruptly. My client was convinced that she'd done a terrible job and spent the next few days agonising over her performance. Only later, after she had got the business, did she learn that the client had been distracted by an important and very personal family matter. It was absolutely nothing to do with her.

## Step 2: Clarify the Issue

You need to be clear about exactly what the sticky situation is before you can do anything about it. If things are at all unclear it's easy to respond in haste to what you *think* is happening. Sometimes comments can be vague, misdirected or exaggerated. So, before you launch into a defence or explanation, take a moment to assess the situation and if necessary, ask for clarification. If you're uncertain, check what has been asked. A good way to do this is by asking what's known as a 'curious' question. For instance: 'I'm curious about where you got that information', or, 'I'm curious about why you feel that way.'

I once sat in on a meeting where the manager complained loudly, saying, 'This information is all wrong.' Immediately one of the others present began to defend the information, explaining the hours of work that had gone into preparing it and the integrity of the data. Half an hour later they discovered that the manager had, in fact, found a couple of minor faults in two of the twelve reports he had been given. He had simply exaggerated, rather than being specific. Had the team member who defended the reports asked exactly what his complaints were, things would have been sorted out much more simply and quickly.

## Step 3: Deal with it Appropriately

Once you understand exactly what is going on, you can respond in the most appropriate way possible. Whatever else you say or do, remain calm and take a deep breath. Count to ten if you need to. Sometimes a few seconds will give you time to come up with a solution, or prevent you from blowing it. Then say or do whatever you think is most likely to get the situation back on track. Make sure you reinforce what you say with your body language. If you want to be firm, stand firm and use a clear voice. And then make sure that your response has addressed the problem and dealt with any criticism or complaint.

There are a number of ways you can choose to respond. You can do it directly by answering the question, or saying so if you don't know. You can put it off until later or pass it to someone else to answer. You can reframe or restate it so that it makes more sense and is easier to answer. Or you can just agree to differ, as in: 'I can appreciate your point of view . . . '

Sometimes all you need to do is to listen attentively, especially if the other person is angry. The fastest way to defuse anger is to listen and acknowledge it.

A senior partner in a retail firm found an error in an invoice from a vendor who was doing some work for the firm. The amount was wrong and he was being overcharged. He talked to the vendor, who launched into a defence of the extra amount, claiming that he was doing extra work, other work he didn't charge for and was working for too little money in the first place. The partner would actually have been happy to pay the extra amount, but the vendor had damaged the relationship with his defensive outburst. Had he dealt with it appropriately by discussing the extra charge in advance and being open and honest about the situation he would have got his money and everyone would have been happy.

### And Remember. . .
The biggest impression you'll make when handling sticky situations will come from how you respond to them and whether you have maintained rapport. Not whether you win or lose but how you play the game. Make it your intention to stay in the ring, physically and emotionally, until the sticky situation is acknowledged and defused.

## THREE TYPES OF STICKY SITUATIONS

As I mentioned earlier on in the chapter, accidents apart, sticky situations fall into three categories:

1. Real and fair objections
2. Odd or mean things other people do
3. Your own little nightmares: things you do to create sticky situations

For each of these categories there are typical situations which you can be prepared for.

### Category One: Real and Fair Objections
These come from the person or people you are meeting and include disagreements, misunderstandings and tough questions. All of these are bound to happen at times, so it's just as well to be familiar with some of the possibilities. Of course, the best way to avoid them is to prepare as thoroughly as possible and to know your subject inside out. That way you can head off all kinds of questions and objections.

Here are some of the most common situations that you might come across.

### When they need more information: the missing link
In this situation you may feel you've given plenty of information, but from your listener's point of view it's not the right kind of information.

This often happens when we overload with information on the basis that more is better. We produce so much that the listener is confused or overwhelmed and simply wants to get to the point that's important to them. Sifting through your information may feel like too much hard work, so you need to do it for them. If someone gets edgy, critical or wants an answer they may not ask directly; instead they might begin to question aspects of what you are talking about, or to ask lots of questions.

### You might hear objections such as

- I'm not sure how this is going to help me improve membership
- This idea sounds very much like something else we are doing
- I don't think you can do what I want
- I can't see how this can happen the way you are proposing it
- I don't know why it costs so much
- Why would it be good to involve John instead of Susan?

They may start looking a bit confused and their eye contact will drift away from you. They may appear to lose interest in what you are saying.

**How to deal with it:** first, get clear about the objection and what you need to clarify. Ask them what information they need – what would make them feel more confident about what you are suggesting or proposing. Don't be shy about what may seem like an obvious question. Then make sure you provide the information as clearly as possible.

**Try this:** before the meeting see whether you can identify the three most important things you *know* your listener may need to know. Write these down and keep them foremost in your message.

### When there is plenty of information, but their understanding or definition of the information is different to yours:- the information clash

Imagine you are at a café following a wonderful night at the theatre, when the waiter asks you, 'How was it?' You answer by telling him the play was marvellous. You even go into a bit of detail about the leading man. Then he says, 'Thanks for that, very interesting, but I meant how was your meal?'

The information 'clash' is really sometimes a matter of definition or positioning. The information is there but it is not offered to them in the way that they want it. Perhaps your emphasis is wrong or there is simply a misunderstanding.

### You might hear an objection such as

- You're talking about providing me with a very personalised and involved service. I just want to have as little of my time spent on this as possible
- I'm looking for a way to cut costs and you are talking about increasing membership
- I don't want you to save me money, that's not the issue; I want a better service

**How to deal with it:** if you hit this kind of clash, then aim to clear up the misunderstanding or to change the emphasis. Answer the specific questions you've been asked and ask the listener if they have the information they need and whether there's anything else they need to know. Be prepared to listen with full attention to what the other person wants to know.

**Try this:** you can prepare before a meeting by knowing ahead of time about a potential clash. For example, you know they might be using a similar service to yours and that you will need to be clear about why yours is better and what you offer that is a bit different.

### When your personal values are different on the subject: the values clash

A value clash happens when your priorities are different or you just don't agree. You can recognise it when the same objection keeps arising regardless of how much information you throw at it or when the listener keeps coming up with different ways to say no to the same point.

### You might hear objections such as

LISTENER:    *I'm afraid it's too expensive.*
YOU:         *I'll give it to you for half price.*
LISTENER:    *It's more than I intended to pay.*
YOU:         *You can pay over three years. . .*
LISTENER:    *No, it still costs too much.*

Or:
YOU:         *We can deliver it on Friday.*
LISTENER:    *No, we will not be home on Friday.*
YOU:         *Well, we can bring it round on Saturday.*
LISTENER:    *I take the kids to sport on Saturday.*
YOU:         *Monday?*
LISTENER:    *I'm visiting a friend on Monday.*

Sometimes this happens because you never really built rapport with the other person. They may feel you just don't 'get' them or didn't demonstrate that you understand what they are about.

Maybe you were too full of jargon, or maybe there is a personal prejudice, or ego is getting in the way.

**How to deal with it:** this kind of resistance usually means that you haven't addressed an important value or need the other person has. It may be that you have to accept defeat, but if they're still willing to talk, ask questions with sensitivity and tact to get to the bottom of the clash. Then, if possible, reassure them with the appropriate information. You may have to put effort into rebuilding rapport that may have been lost.

**Try this:** if you're really poles apart, and you're not getting anywhere, suggest that you will take time after the meeting to explore alternatives that they may find acceptable.

### Category Two: Odd or Mean Things People Do

People sometimes behave in ways that lead us to think that they're being odd or mean, whether they intend to or not. Behaviour can often appear mean when it isn't intended to be. This might include the person who wanders around the room or picks up a newspaper as you speak, the person who talks across you, yells, laughs, sleeps, sneaks looks at their watch or puts their feet on the desk. It might also include the person who asks a deliberately disruptive or critical question or who comments negatively as you speak.

Why do people use a tactic like this? Often to unnerve you and get you to lower your expectations so that they can get a better deal or feel more powerful. It can also be what they consider to be normal behaviour for them. Don't judge too quickly.

These behaviours, and many other similar ones, can also be mischievous, nervous, or even innocent. But whatever the intent behind them, they can be unnerving.

**How to deal with it:** behaviours like this can be upsetting, but the cardinal rule is, don't take it personally. All it tells you is that the other person is rude, unaware, mean or eccentric.

Check to make sure that you're not doing anything to provoke the behaviour, such as running over time. If not, then keep a grip on the situation by keeping cool and, if appropriate, carrying on. The behaviour might well be designed to test you, so the less nervous you appear and the more calmly you are able to go on, the more brownie points you'll be notching up.

Whatever else you do, keep your sense of humour; it's vital in this kind of situation.

**Try this:** identify the types of behaviour that really unnerve or upset you. For instance, you may be reasonably OK with people yelling but get thrown by impatient sighing, or vice versa. Or you may get really hot under the collar about people who don't listen and pay attention, or who interrupt. Prepare yourself by thinking through the kinds of situations you know can unnerve you and being ready for them. Remember that sometimes it's just a nervous reaction from the other person and that even if it's a deliberate tactic, it can only be as powerful as you let it be.

Here are some alternative ways you could respond to odd or mean behaviour:

- Ignore it, especially if it's someone falling asleep
- Acknowledge it and ask the person politely if everything is OK
- Accommodate it by shifting your attention to where the person has moved to in the room
- Use humour. Sometimes this will break the tension in a room and create a more relaxed environment
- Take a break

- Subtly let the other person know that you're aware of what they're doing, through pauses, eye contact, moving closer to them or asking them for any comments or suggestions. This will shift the focus to them
- Refuse to continue if the behaviour is genuinely disruptive. No one expects you to take abuse

Don't be tempted to embarrass the person, stoop to their level or be a petty schoolteacher by asking them to 'share with the group'. Keep your dignity in place and resist pettiness.

Whatever the disruption you can gain ground by holding your ground physically. Make sure you don't step back, cross your arms, tilt your head back or lose eye contact. Stay present and connected and let the person who is disrupting things finish. Leave a pause to be sure they really have finished, rather than jumping straight in to try to solve what you think is the problem. Sometimes just showing that you can stay quiet and listen will go a long way towards putting things right. If you're facilitating a meeting then it's your duty to get things back on track, so don't be shy to acknowledge that the meeting has moved off schedule.

### Category Three: Your Own Little Nightmares

This category is about the things we can all do that create sticky situations. Even the most cautious and careful person can blow it every now and then. Sometimes it is just 'your foot that kicked the brick that hit the baby on the head' – accidents happen. But at other times it can be lack of skill, sheer terror or inexperience that causes the problem.

Although you can never guarantee to avoid all sticky moments, you can certainly reduce the odds by knowing what the most common pitfalls are.

These are some of the ones I have seen most often:

- **Making lots of little mistakes:** this is usually the result of
  nerves or poor preparation. Prepare well and if you're likely to
  be very nervous take steps to help yourself. A sip of water, a
  deep breath, a smile or a short break can all help
- **Acting surprised and making up answers:** if you do this
  people will know immediately and you'll look pretty silly. If
  you're asked something you can't answer be honest about it
  and say you'll find out. Then do it
- **Blaming others and defending ourselves:** never blame
  others or defend yourself, it just makes you look bad. If you
  catch yourself doing this, stop immediately
- **Getting the facts wrong:** if you realise you've made this
  mistake then apologise and rectify it as quickly as possible
- **Waffling:** if you find yourself waffling or rambling you'll lose
  your listener's interest fast. Stop and get back on track. A
  useful way to do this is to say you'll give a brief summary of
  what's been said/agreed so far
- **Misreading the style of the listener:** I once watched a firm
  of architects dressed in pastel linen suits use flamboyant
  language to describe the modernistic lobby design they
  proposed to a group of grey, grim-faced bankers. No, they
  didn't get the contract. They didn't even finish the
  presentation. Avoid this mistake by doing your research in
  advance
- **Losing control:** this can happen if others take over while
  you're talking. It can mess up your timing and hurt your
  credibility. Get the focus back to you by asking whether
  everyone is still on track with the initial agreement of 'what
  we're here to discuss and how we're going to achieve it'.
  You can also mention the time as a constraint; this
  sometimes results in everyone agreeing immediately to
  get back on track
- **Interrupting others:** if you do this, people will feel you're rude
  and not listening to them. Get a grip, stop and say, 'Excuse

me. Please go on with what you were saying.' Over time, start catching yourself before you interrupt. If you legitimately need to interrupt, raise your hand to about shoulder level and address the person by name. For instance: 'Karen, excuse me, but due to time constraints we have to get back on track'

- **Losing your cool:** if you find yourself getting rattled or joining in a shouting match then take a break, get out of the room, breathe deeply and wait until you feel fully in control before going back in

Most of the sticky situations you may find yourself in can either be avoided in the first place, by preparing thoroughly and responding appropriately, or easily defused, by keeping cool and refusing to take things personally or become flustered.

## GET-LOST LINES

Get-lost lines create a special kind of sticky situation. They often come out of the blue and leave you feeling foolish, tongue-tied or panicking. They're the disheartening 'no' lines that you can get when approaching someone for a meeting or in the meeting when you land one. If you let them, they can leave you feeling flat and wondering why you bothered.

Here are the top lines I've heard:

- Send me a proposal and I'll think about it
- Things take a long time in this place. Nothing I can do about it
- That sounds really interesting, let me get back to you
- We don't have a budget for this
- We/I don't have any money to do this
- I've heard this idea before. We've already decided not to do it
- Let's talk again next year
- I'll call you next week after I've had a meeting with so-and-so
- No thanks. I'm not interested
- You've got the wrong person

- Why don't you leave some stuff with me and I'll read it and get back to you
- We have a group meeting in a few weeks where this stuff will be discussed. I'll get back to you after that
- I'm too busy
- This is too expensive
- Have you thought about doing something else?

The important thing to remember when you hear any of these lines, or any others like them, is that they don't usually mean a flat 'no' at all. They're often simply distractions, aimed at lowering your expectations, testing you or giving the other person the upper hand.

Take money, for instance. They might say, 'There's no money for this,' but if that were really true there wouldn't be a meeting in the first place. There's always money to be spent, even if it isn't immediately.

So, when you hear lines like these, don't be discouraged. Persevere by making fresh suggestions or asking for another meeting at a later date.

## AND FINALLY . . .

Sticky situations are a part of life, sometimes unavoidable, often hilarious (afterwards) and there to test us. If you can accept that you're bound to come up against a few of them then you'll be less surprised when they come along. And if you can keep your cool and deal with them with a little compassion and wisdom and plenty of humour, then rather than losing face you'll come through them looking great and feeling even better.

# 10

# FIXING THE PHYSICAL

*What is music? Music is what happens*
*between the notes*
**LEONARD BERNSTEIN**

Every time you walk into a room where there are other
people, they will form an impression of what kind of person
you are before you say your first word. Body language, as I
mentioned in the chapter on rapport, creates over half of the
impression we make on others. No matter how clever, well-
rehearsed and impressive your words are, they will only ever
be part of the picture you create in the minds of others.

That's why it's vital to pay attention to the physical
impression you make on others. I see people every day who
give an impression they didn't intend, without meaning to.
They wonder what they did 'wrong', why someone didn't
seem to like them or didn't give them the business, the job or
the sponsorship. They feel they've been judged unfairly.

The trouble is that once someone has formed an impression of you it doesn't matter whether that impression is right
or not. There can be a great big gap between the way you
come across to others and the way you'd *like* to come across,
but changing the impression once it's been made can be very

hard work indeed. So, putting a bit of effort into making the 'right' impression in the first place is well worth working on.

The impressions we create are important enough for big business to care about. A friend of mine is a well-respected forensic anthropologist in the United States and for many years her job was to 'observe' jurors during the course of major trials. She would watch their expressions, posture, movement and reactions and give feedback to the lawyers about which jurors she believed were being convinced or not and on which issues. This allowed the lawyers to adjust their evidence and emphasis and helped to make her legal team extremely successful.

You too can up your success rate by paying attention to body language – yours and other people's. In this chapter I'm going to look at the unspoken impressions we make on others, how exactly we make these impressions and what we can do to make the best impression possible.

After that I'll go on to look at the way we observe others and how you can start to notice the unspoken signals others give you. This will give you a great advantage when it comes to choosing your response to them.

## THE MESSAGES YOU GIVE

Every day we give out unspoken messages to other people. Even someone who sees you in the street or sitting on a train will form an impression of you. They'll notice whether you look tired, full of energy, sad or bored. They'll also notice whether you're smartly dressed or scruffy and whether your hair is neat or a mess. But these obvious things are just the start of what someone observing you for a few minutes would notice. There are many other more subtle actions, expressions and signals that they would pick up.

Stephanie Burns is an author and educator who has spent

twenty years studying adults and has come up with something she calls 'Seven Observable Behaviours'. She has
identified seven main types of behaviours that people
observe to form impressions about us.

These seven behaviours are:

1. Dress
2. Facial expression
3. Voice
4. Gestures
5. Posture
6. Movement
7. Energy levels

Observing behaviour involves picking up on a range of
signals and creating a bigger picture by putting them
together. We all do this naturally all the time. We're capable
of unconsciously processing vast amounts of information
and, without ever analysing the detail, making decisions and
judgements about other people based on this information.

It follows that, when you're aiming for success, you will
want to create a great impression in the minds of those you
are communicating with.

So, let's go through those seven behaviours and look at
how each one makes an impression and what you can do to
choose the kind of impression you make.

## 1. Dress
It's important to dress appropriately for the situation. Do
you wear your chunky diamond bracelet and gold watch to
the Salvation Army fund-raising meeting? Do you wear your
favourite ancient fertility symbol, feather earrings and giant
hammer-and-sickle belt buckle to visit your conservative
bank manager? You get the picture. Be aware of the impression you create.

I've witnessed countless errors of judgment around appearance that could so easily have been avoided with a little foresight and research.

There is no right and wrong about the way you dress and look; what's right for one situation may not be right for another. But image consultants tend to agree that it's better to be subtle and play down distractions. Walk into a room with bright pink hair, a micro-skirt, a multicoloured tie or an armful of bracelets and the focus will immediately be on you, for all the reasons you may not want. Dress like this and you may take away from the effectiveness of your communication and end up working twice as hard to get your message across.

I had a conservative American client who once said: 'Everything that is not necessary is an affectation.' This is a useful rule to apply to the way you dress because it's almost always better to under-do it than to over-do it.

Don't forget about accessories either. Many people feel naked without their accessories, others uncomfortable with them. My personal view is that less is better, but I've been accused of being very American and under-accessorised when I visit my Italian clients. (Just watch me try to do that scarf-thing European women do and you'll see why I avoid it. I look as though I've got the results of a nasty accident draped around my neck.)

Notice the small things. One client told me of a team of actuaries who were presenting for new business. One of the presenters had her sunglasses on top of her head. The message the clients took from that was that she was just too hip and would rather be having a cappuccino on the terrace than be in this meeting. It seems harmless enough and was probably unintentional, but it caused a lot of damage.

Exposing too much flesh is another high-risk area. There are still women out there who let the sisterhood down by overtly flashing inappropriate bits of female flesh in the wrong situations. Very short skirts, lots of cleavage and exposed bellies all bring about a heterosexual male response that doesn't amount to listening, so unless your subject is about the beauty of exposing female flesh, try to avoid it.

Finally, make sure that what you're wearing is clean and fits properly: too tight or even too big never looks good and grubby is even worse.

I remember being asked to make a presentation to a group of senior partners at a posh Los Angeles law firm. The very kind man who was sponsoring me took one look at my shoes and took me down to the shoeshine man before he would let me in through the door. Embarrassing, but a good lesson. Always do a triple check before entering a room.

## 2. Facial Expression

You facial expression is a very important part of how you communicate, yet so many of us cover our faces with glasses, hair and make-up.

The most common cover-up for women is hair that falls over the face, particularly in presentations when they're looking down at notes. It comes across as a kind of protective shield and implies immaturity or lack of confidence even if what you're actually doing is trying to be sexy. Much better to have hair off the face and if it's long, tied back in such a way that it won't distract.

Heavy make-up is a personal choice, but under pressure, when you get hotter or the lights are bright, it can become a sloppy mess, so take care.

Men who have facial hair need to be aware that by the time they have a beard and moustache in full bloom there is only about 30 per cent of their face left to look at. Facial hair also becomes something to fiddle with, pinch and stroke. There are too many prejudices about facial hair for it to be a safe option, but if you're willing to bear the slings and arrows, at least keep it neat.

Glasses are fine as long as people can still see your eyes. Swap heavy, dark frames for light ones, and if you can choose non-reflective glass, that's even better.

Lastly, remember to look cheerful. It lightens the atmosphere and creates an instant bond. I had a client say to one of his poker-faced colleagues once: 'If you're happy, tell your face!'

## 3. Voice

I have a friend who is the Master of Voice at Shakespeare's Globe Theatre in London. He thinks about the power of the voice in a way that most of us wouldn't even dream of. 'Voices are the windows of our souls,' he says. 'Not just our wilful servants.'

You can use your voice not just to get your message across but to affect your listeners in powerful ways. You can tease, calm, play, frighten, amuse, inform, persuade. The voice is a versatile, personal and wondrous tool – and an important vehicle for building relationships.

When we like the sound of a person's voice it's because it sounds smooth, sultry, expressive, clear or melodious. A pleasant voice can be a joy to listen to. On the other hand, an annoying voice is really hard to listen to for any length of time. Annoying voices are often described as nasal or squeaky, hoarse, too loud or too soft.

When a person's voice becomes an issue and sounds jarring, instead of resonating pleasantly, it is a reflection of that person's state of mind and physical condition.

The key to having a good strong and clear voice lies in the way you breathe. If you're not breathing properly, naturally and deeply, then you're creating some sound other than your full, authentic voice.

There are two very common problems, both connected to bad breathing, that affect the voice. The first is a tight neck and tongue, which creates either a nasal sound, a high squeaky voice or a voice that is too loud or too soft. The other is pushing your voice down to create authority – it can make the voice monotonous. Both these habits put stress on your vocal chords and rob you of that wonderful natural sound that is your own voice.

The solution is to correct your breathing. We often adopt poor breathing habits as a result of anxiety and tension, which tighten and constrict the chest. This is a little like squeezing a full balloon at the neck to let puffs of air out at a time.

Here are some simple exercises to help you breathe better and create a more natural voice:

- Start by breathing from your diaphragm – your solar plexus. Imagine filling your lungs like a glass of water. Feel your ribs opening and breathe into your belly. Relax your shoulders and let your arms hang loose. Do this as often as you can and need to. Slowly, don't rush it. Find your own rhythm
- Your voice tone communicates confidence and credibility. Try this exercise to improve your tone: start to hum and feel the hum through your nose, your chest and all the way into your belly. While you are humming, feel the buzz on your lips. Relax your throat and neck and shoulders. Find the most natural sound you can make
- The voice has a wonderful range of notes yet most of the time we only use a narrow range. Try making it louder and softer. Experiment with emphasis. Be a little more animated and interesting
- Articulation is the clarity with which you pronounce your words. This is one of the exercises I use to help clients who are preparing to make major speeches. To loosen up those

articulation muscles say 'wee-wah' repeatedly. Exaggerate your facial expressions on each word. Relax your neck. This exercise is for your face and mouth.

- Then try an exercise we used to use at Rogen. Say 'you-you-you' repeatedly in a pouty-kissy-lipped motion and repeat each word quickly.

- Now massage the cheeks and pronounce the sounds:
    Te with the tip of the tongue
    Ke with the middle of the tongue
    Ge with the back of the tongue

- Finally say 'HA-HA-HA' distinctly and loudly. Send each HA to different parts of the room. See what it feels like to 'talk' to different parts of a big room

Try these exercises daily to improve your breathing and the tone and range of your voice. Remember that your voice is your representative, particularly when you're talking on the phone. People will learn a great deal about you from your voice and will respond to what they hear. Make yours warm, clear, interesting and inviting.

## 4. Gestures

Our hands are our body's punctuation and exclamation marks. They add emphasis and flavour to what we are saying. If you're comfortable with what to do with them they can be a source of natural expression and a wonderful visual aid.

On the other hand, if you're uncomfortable, your hands can create a distraction. This can happen when someone is the focus of attention or under pressure. I've had many people tell me that in nervous situations they feel as if their hands don't belong to them any more. They suddenly seem larger than life or do distracting things they would never normally do. 'What am I doing with my hands? I didn't know I did that!' is often the comment when people watch a video replay of themselves presenting.

Gesturing is a form of energy, so higher-energy people tend to do it more, lower-energy people tend to do it less. The amount you gesture depends on your own particular style, but bear in mind also the context and the people you're talking to. For instance – and I know I'm generalising here – the Italians would find it strange if you didn't gesture a lot, while the Japanese would find it strange if you did.

Three things to keep in mind about your hands:

1. The key to natural gesturing is to know how to rest your hands. Once you get the hang of this, everything else will fall into place. By resting, I mean being comfortable with what you're doing with your hands when you aren't using them.
   This is a good place to rest your hands when the spotlight is on you: stand up and put your hands in a relaxed position hanging at your sides. Relax your neck and shoulders. Now bend your arms at the elbow with your hands facing forward at 45 degrees. Keep your elbows relaxed and close to your body. Put your hands together in front of you at waist height, clasping them gently together.
   You may have seen the weather forecaster doing this on TV! It's very relaxed and neutral and your hands are ready when you want to gesture.
   If you're seated, rest your hands on top of the table, folded neatly over each other.
2. When you use your hands, be definite about it. By being definite, I mean choose to use your hands to help clarify and emphasise your messages. Start the gesture and finish it rather than letting it tail off. If you're going to do it, do it.
   Be aware if you tend to gesture all the time. Get selective. It gets difficult to tell what you think is important if your hands are moving constantly. Gesturing without a break can also

affect the pace at which you speak, and act as a metronome. If you speak too quickly, check to see that you're not also gesturing all the time. Try to minimise the gesturing and see if it helps you slow down. When you're preparing a talk or presentation, think about places where a gesture would help you emphasise your point. Practise the gesture and if it feels right, use it.

3. Think about pushing yourself a little. In my experience, most people tend to under-gesture awkwardly rather than over-gesture. If this is you then experiment a little. Break out of your comfort zone. If you're speaking in front of a large group you need to make your gestures a little bigger, purely because of the distance between you and your listeners. Begin to enjoy your hands as a form of expression, a useful aid to what you want to say.

## 5. Posture and Movement

I've put these two together because they're so closely linked. Our posture and the way we move give a message that we send out even when we're not thinking about it. We can tell from someone's posture whether they are feeling good, happy and full of energy, or tired and low.

Bad posture is incredibly common. We develop it over the years through lack of awareness about our bodies, lack of exercise, or the wrong exercise, bad chairs, poor health, low self-confidence or just being tired. Few of us know how much our posture affects our energy levels and the way we think and feel.

The good thing is that by adjusting your posture and movement, which you can do quite easily with a little effort, you will also start to make subtle changes to your attitude. Change your posture or move in a new way and it will immediately make you feel different. It's a great illustration of the power of the mind-body link.

I once worked with a client who was being considered for promotion to partner at a major law firm in the United States. His colleagues called me in because although he was considered intelligent, capable and worthy of partnership, they felt he didn't seem to have the energy or dynamism to deal with CEO-level clients of major multinationals. He often seemed to fade into the wallpaper during meetings, saying very little.

Having met him, I realised a number of things were sending the physical messages 'low-energy'. He was quite tall but had a 'lazy middle'. In other words, he had slightly rounded shoulders and his arms dangled at his sides almost pulling his shoulders and ribcage down. This also made his chest slightly concave and created the impression that he had a huge weight on his shoulders.

His posture affected the speed at which he walked, causing him to appear to shuffle along. He was also short-sighted, making him look down for long periods and bend towards the table. All this physical pulling 'downwards' affected his ability to stay in a dynamic conversation and to pay attention. I discovered he also had a high-sugar diet, which compounded his low energy levels at certain times of the day.

We set out on a campaign of fixing the physical things that were creating this impression. He had to learn to stand properly, to rest and to develop a more natural and energetic way of carrying himself. Retraining his muscles took him about three months and during this time he also changed his bad eating habits. By the end he had a higher level of energy generally, walked with a spring in his step and looked more attentive and interested. Soon afterwards he left that firm to become a partner at another firm. He also met a new girlfriend!

Men and women have different bad posture habits. The most common male ones are often the result of an effort to appear authoritative. They include having very square rigid shoulders, squaring-off the whole body with equal weight on both feet and facing forward in an almost military way, hands covering the crotch (like a fig-leaf) or else on hips. These postures create an impression of discipline, rigidity and force.

Women, on the other hand, tend to have their weight slightly off-balance, legs crossed (while standing or seated), head slightly tilted, hands low and behind the back. These postures can create an impression of flexibility, vulnerability and submissiveness.

Notice your posture and ask others around you to tell you what they see you doing. Try sitting, standing and walking differently, with extra energy and in a more upright way.

A useful posture tip is to try using the 'forward and back' space. You can affect the way you feel and behave and the way you use it will affect those around you as well.

Leaning forward is considered a 'tell, push, eager, inter-ested' position, while leaning back is an 'ask, listen, think, placate' position. Notice what you're doing when you're listening or telling someone something. Where is your body?

A friend of mine was told that she was creating a dis-traction by leaning forward too eagerly as she was listening. When she leaned forward she started to interrupt and finish people's sentences so that other people felt she wasn't really listening. She also breathed more rapidly.

I asked her to try leaning back slightly while others were talking and to rest in that position. She soon noticed that in this new position she found it easier to listen without inter-rupting and breathed more slowly.

## 6 Energy Levels

Everyone would love to have that special something we call charisma. To be the person who walks into a room and appears effortlessly attractive and charming, so that everyone around is drawn to them. Charisma is a kind of personal energy that goes beyond words. Its role in our ability to persuade others is powerful. Yet charisma is not mysterious or unavailable. It's not one of those things that you've either got or you haven't. Charisma is something you can cultivate, because the secret behind it is intention combined with communication skills.

I've seen people work really hard at 'having' charisma. They walk into a room and move from person to person like a bee in a garden – shaking hands, standing tall and smiling. Yet something is wrong, they don't have the desired effect. That's because they're too busy thinking about themselves and the way they're coming across. Doing this, they have very little energy left for the person they're talking to. We've all talked to someone like this. You feel awkward because their eyes are wandering over your shoulder, they're not really listening to what you say and you can tell they want to move on to the next person.

Now take someone who really does have charisma. I have a friend who is a well-known figure and is often a speaker and guest at events around the world. I asked various people why they felt he was so wonderful – what is it about him? Every person commented on how they felt as if he was really listening to them, as though theirs was the only conversation in the room. This man put his focus totally on that person for the time they were together and they felt special.

Then I watched him 'work a room' to see what he was doing to make people feel so special. What I noticed was that there was nothing artificial about his contact with people. He stood close enough to block outside interference into the conversation, made good eye contact, always shook hands and had a laugh. Most significant of all, the other person was always talking more.

One of the biggest secrets of this man's success, and this applies to most people with charisma, was that he knew how to listen – one of the most powerful communication skills of all.

It's easy to give the impression that you're not listening, and nothing puts others off more quickly. So, make an effort to listen, *really* listen, to what each person is saying.

My friend also had intention, the other key ingredient of charisma. Intention is defined as showing earnest or eager attention. It's the energy behind what you are, it moves you forward and it shows in your body language. Intention is the stuff you radiate, and when it's strong, it acts like a magnet to others.

Developing your intention is valuable in all sorts of ways. It can be a way to overcome nervousness and take the focus off yourself, as well as the key to creating charisma.

So, how do you do it? Here's a useful guide:

- When you walk into a room, leave your baggage outside the door. There is nothing else. Only that moment
- Believe that there's something interesting in everyone and look for it
- Believe that you have something each person can benefit from, namely, your energy and interest. Think of your energy and interest as a bright light that runs through you – head to toe – and is radiating out as you walk into the room
- Mix into that a genuine desire to succeed and give as much good as you can to each person. I'm not talking about wandering around blessing each person and anointing them with oil. At least, not overtly. Just with your intent. Sounds like a foolish thing to do after a hard day's work? Not really. In fact, it is the best thing you can do for yourself. It will invigorate you and you'll enjoy the effect it has on others

This example sums up what fixing the physical is really about:

My colleague Phyllis was one of the first people I hired to set up our office in the United States. She came highly recommended, she was professional, intelligent and already successful in her own right. Yet in the first six months we received consistent comments from potential clients about how young and inexperienced she appeared. We couldn't understand why people weren't responding to her in the way we wanted, so we decided to find out what she was doing to create this wrong impression and came up with three things.

1. Phyllis always wore dangly earrings that hung about an inch below the bottom of her ear. When she stopped moving her head the earrings kept swinging and this created a kind of 'little girl dressed up', slightly comical impression.
2. When Phyllis spoke, she tended to gesture in small circles with her little finger splayed out and this looked quite child-like.
3. When she was in meetings, Phyllis had the amazing ability to take longhand notes without looking at the page. Even though she knew what she was doing, clients couldn't imagine that what she was writing – without looking – could be very important, and it was incredibly distracting to watch her do it.

As soon as Phyllis changed these three habits, the comments about her inexperience and youth stopped. It was that simple.

## GET COMFORTABLE WITH SILENCE

Most of us are uncomfortable with silence – and it shows. We fidget, break eye contact, shift our posture, clear our throat and withdraw our attention. These physical reactions can be very unsettling, both to ourselves and to others around us. So, becoming comfortable with silence is an important part of creating the right physical impact.

Too often we jump in with something to say, rather than

allow a silence and the discomfort it brings. I've often noticed that silence after a question has been asked is very difficult for some people to handle. If I pause before my answer, the person opposite me will often feel the need to 'rescue' me by commenting. In contrast, silence after a statement has been made often compels the person who made the statement to say more. Amazing the effect it has on most of us.

Yet silence is not just emptiness or the absence of sound. It's often a point of creativity and breakthrough. Out of silence can come new beginnings and greater understanding. Silence can feel good, interesting and wondrous.

Culture plays a big part in our comfort levels and familiarity with silence. A cross-cultural survey done in 1976 by Ishii and Knopf showed the average person in the USA talks twice as long each day as the average person in Japan (6 hours and 43 minutes compared to 3 hours and 31 minutes). The average Westerner speaks first, listens second and observes third (ready, fire, aim). In Eastern culture there is a different preference: observe, listen, speak.

A Japanese friend told me about 'enryo-sasshi'. The Japanese tend to simplify their messages and avoid long verbal elaboration of their ideas because they rely on the listener's intuition to 'get' the meaning. It is considered rude to talk too much because you are not showing sensitivity to the other's 'enryo' (ability to get it). If you are good at 'sasshi', then you are good at perceiving the whole message through the context, the body language and tone. If you do this you will be perceived as wisdom-seeking and open-minded.

You can help yourself get more comfortable with silence by practising it. Notice what happens to your body when you feel compelled to fill a silent space and try to do something different.

Learning to meditate is the best way to increase your comfort with silence. Find out which kind of meditation suits you and your lifestyle and make it part of your daily routine.

Choose silence more often. It can be very productive. Start with something as simple as a visit to a coffee shop or a park without something to read or someone to talk to. Just sit. Observe. See how it feels. Resist the temptation to turn on the TV or radio when you have a moment alone. Walk or exercise without headphones or your mobile phone. Eat without reading the newspaper. A wise old man I met said, 'If you're going to eat, eat. If you're going to walk, walk.'

As you become more comfortable with silence, you will begin to notice more about others around you. Your relationships will be richer because you've let silence create time for understanding others. You can see more with your mouth closed and your eyes open.

## DEALING WITH NERVES

Make a friend of nervousness. If you do, you can use the heightened state of awareness to work for you. Being nervous helps you prepare better, gives you energy and can focus you, whereas when it takes control of you, embarrassing things can happen. Don't judge or get angry with yourself for feeling nervous. Go with it and let it pass. The more you resist it the more it hangs around.

Nervousness happens for two main reasons:

1. You need more success under your belt. So often people are nervous because they just haven't clocked up enough 'good' experiences. The remedy is to throw yourself into the ring more often. Nothing replaces just getting out there and doing it. You feel better if you've done something well a few times. Put some memory in your muscles!
2. You get taken by surprise. There are all kinds of surprises that can throw us off track. For instance, people you didn't expect

show up at a meeting, your technology breaks down, you (or someone else) spill, drop, smudge, explode, erase, forget, panic or mess up in some way. Expect anything. The best remedy for surprise is to minimise it by rehearsing and making yourself as familiar as you can with the surroundings and the people before you get into the spotlight. Sounds simple, but you'd be surprised at how many people don't make the effort and end up being surprised.

Nervous distractions are pretty obvious to your listener and common to all of us, and the rub is that we often don't know when they are happening to us.

Here are some of the most common:

- Red, splotchy neck (most common in women)
- Jiggling leg (most common in men)
- Shaky hands
- Squeaky/choked-up/awkward voice
- Waffling
- Pacing up and down
- Speed talking

If you find yourself doing any of these things, then make yourself aware, forgive yourself and work out a way to stop it. The most helpful thing you can do is slow down and take a deep breath – sounds simple, but most of us aren't breathing properly when these things happen.

## OBSERVING OTHERS

As we learn to notice ourselves we also begin to notice others in more detail. Of course, we do make quick assessments of each other, but this is not always a good thing. Sometimes these impressions get us out of danger or get us into wonderful new experiences. But sometimes first impressions can dig us a hole so deep we don't have a shovel big enough to get out.

When you form impressions about others you won't always be right; the key is getting it right more often. And to do this you need to reserve judgement, take your time and seek more information. Don't guess at what the whole painting looks like by looking only at the lower left-hand corner.

One of the best things you can do for yourself is to learn to listen to and look after your body. It will make you more able to observe others accurately and fairly. Your body will tell you when you don't trust or like something, when you should run away and when you should stay. I was told by one of the world's most successful physicians never to provoke the body. It is a force to be reckoned with and it always wins. Listen to it.

If we're looking through observant eyes we can see when people are feeling ill, uncomfortable, shy, happy or sad as well as when they're being honest or dishonest with us. You don't have to work that hard to see some of these things such as energy levels, posture, facial expression and movement. You know how difficult it is to keep yourself from blushing if you're embarrassed, smiling if you're happy or excited, or from shaking, or being tense and dry-mouthed when you are truly nervous. Use what you have learned about your own reactions and physical expressions to know and understand others better, to read situations and to respond effectively and appropriately.

# 11

# CHANCE MEETINGS

*Chance favours the prepared mind*
**LOUIS PASTEUR**

Meeting people by chance is something that happens all the time. We bump into someone in the supermarket, playground, wine bar or station and get chatting. Mostly we walk away having had a pleasant encounter and forget all about it. But chance meetings can be a valuable opportunity when it comes to achieving your goal.

Many of my clients have told me that they made their best contacts at chance meetings. The head of a major bank has done fifteen years worth of business with a man he met on a beach in Spain. An art gallery owner had his most successful-ever exhibition after sitting next to a bright young artist on a plane.

Think of your own life and the people who mean most to you. Where and when did you meet them? It's very likely that a good number of them came into your life by chance. Often the best things happen when you least expect them.

One friend of mine met the woman who now looks after her children on a bus. Before they met, my friend had gone through endless problems with childcare. The woman on the bus happened to be looking for a job and has turned out to be the best carer my friend has ever em[ployed. My friend, her husband, her children, the carer and her family are all better off as a result of this chance meeting.

Friends often arrive in our lives through chance meetings. A headteacher I know told me that she met her closest friend in a supermarket. They got chatting over the frozen veg, decided they clicked in the toiletries aisle and arranged to meet for coffee while queuing at the checkout. That was twenty years ago.

If you know how to take advantage of a chance meeting and use it wisely, it can be of enormous value. But for every chance meeting that bears fruit, another twenty opportunities are lost. Some people are too shy or self-conscious to start chatting, even when they get a friendly smile of invitation. The thought of talking to a stranger can be nerve-racking and is a major cause of social anxiety that plenty of people would rather just bypass.

For other people it isn't fear that stops them. They simply walk around with their heads in the clouds, deep in thought and totally unaware of the possibilities for contact with people around them. We've all had times when we walk past someone we know well without noticing them, just because we're so distracted. Looking out for chance meetings and handling them well is something you can choose to do. That's why I've included chance meetings in the persusavive 'toolbox'. They present a golden opportunity that too many people run away from, ignore or are simply unaware of.

To help you take advantage of the wonderful possibilities chance meetings offer, I'm going to give you some practical guidelines for starting conversations and building rapport with people you haven't expected to meet. Once you're aware of the opportunities around you and willing to engage with others, then chance meetings will become another valuable tool you can use to improve your ability to be a persuasive communicator and achieve your goals.

## CHANCE VERSUS NETWORKING

Most people in the world of business know about networking: attending highly organised and carefully planned meetings, gatherings and social occasions with the intention of making useful contacts, sharing ideas and furthering business opportunities.

A lot of money and effort on the part of companies and individuals goes into networking. Yet when I did my own survey about the difference between the quality of relationships that sprang out of active networking versus chance meetings, 90 per cent of the clients I asked said that their best, longest and most productive business relationships came from meetings that were not expected. In other words, chance meetings.

Many people spend a large portion of their lives attending dinners, lunches and social conventions of one sort or another, for the simple reason that meeting and connecting with others is vital to their success. It's hard work and only seasoned players stay the course and keep at it year after year.

Of course, networking can be extremely useful. Good contacts are made, deals are done, information shared. But meetings that happen purely by chance, with no planning at all, are just as useful, if not more so.

Since you can't plan a chance meeting, there's no point worrying about them or wondering if you'll ever get one. Believe me, everyone has them. That's why it's so important to be on the look-out for them and ready to gain the most from them when they happen.

Chance meetings happen while you're getting on with life. Going shopping, taking your kids out, going on holiday, waiting for a train.

We all spend a lot of time doing these things. That's why the chance of having a useful chance meeting is pretty high! These everyday activities are fertile ground for some of the most interesting and important relationships you can have.

## BE OPEN TO THE POSSIBILITIES

The key to chance meetings is your attitude towards them. First of all, you don't make chance meetings happen, you let them happen. So, forget about trying to control events and begin by being relaxed about the whole thing. When you stop expecting it or trying to engineer it, a chance meeting will come along.

When it does, don't kill it with over-enthusiasm. Relax and be willing to learn. If you're determined to get something out of it you'll appear pushy and nothing is more off-putting. Be warm, enthusiastic and genuine. Take an interest in the other person. Forget about pursuing your dream or goal and pursue warm, enjoyable contact. Chance meetings are not the place for selling or doing deals. The most important take-away from a chance meeting is not what you both said but how you both felt after you met. People remember meetings they enjoyed.

An advertising executive was made redundant and decided to retrain as an educational psychologist. To do this he needed a psychology degree, which he had, and teaching experience, which he didn't have. He applied for a job as a classroom assistant but was turned down.

A couple of weeks later he got chatting to a woman he met while taking his children swimming. They got on well, his children liked hers and she invited him and his family over to her house for a play session the following weekend. Only at this second meeting did he discover that she was a head teacher with a vacancy in her school for a classroom assistant. And having talked to him about a wide range of subjects and seen how good he was with children, she was only too happy to employ him.

Don't think of the person you meet by chance as a stranger. After all, you're in the same situation so you already have something in common. That's a great place to start.

If you build up enough of the right kind of rapport then you'll be able to follow up the chance meeting at a later date. And when you welcome chance meetings and learn from them, amazing things start happening.

I have a great friend, Julie, who often meets someone by chance who is in some way remotely or otherwise connected to someone else in her life. Ten years ago she sat next to someone on an aeroplane from Bangkok to Los Angeles and happened to mention the name of a designer she hoped to meet. The person she'd sat next to knew this designer and arranged to introduce them. Julie got on really well with the designer and they planned to do some work together. The designer knew me and introduced me to Julie. We've been good friends ever since.

## BE WILLING TO ENGAGE

If you want a chance meeting to work in your favour you must be willing to engage with the other person.

Engaging involves body language and conversation. If you are warm, smiling, willing to listen and to talk, and interested in the other person then you're engaging well.

Peter Rogen, whom I once worked with, identified four

levels of engagement. And while we all use all of them at times, we can usually identify one that we use most often.

Read the description of each and ask yourself which ones you recognise and which you are most likely to use when you have a chance encounter.

Level One        Engaging to be Polite: I'm hearing but not listening. I may be smiling and nodding and looking at you but I'm really thinking about when this conversation will be over or about my shopping list. Probably won't remember your name. Ho-hum. I'm probably looking over your shoulder, too.

Level Two        Engaging to be Right: I know what you're going to say – I might even finish your sentences. As long as you say what I want to hear I'll keep listening. I'm doing a mental check all the time, ticking the boxes against my interests and I'm usually judging whether you know what you're talking about. I'll probably interject and correct so that you know my point of view. My brain is busy keeping tabs only on what I want to hear. I'm good at drawing conclusions about people and you're next.

Level Three      Engaging Selectively: I have a pretty good idea about how I want this chance meeting to turn out because I know what you do for a living and it relates to what I do. There could be a good business or personal opportunity here. I'll listen for the things you say that would allow me the excuse to see you at your office next week. I'm going to make a mental note of it as soon as I hear it. Let's only talk about or steer the conversation towards what is beneficial either to me or to both of us.

Level Four     Engaging to Learn: I want to understand as much as possible about you in the time available and under the circumstances. Let's enjoy this chance meeting. I want to know what interests you and the things we may have in common other than the fact that we are here now. I'm interested beyond work opportunity or personal gain. I'm doing my best not to cloud my mind by judging or looking for right or wrong. I'm listening more than I'm talking.

Level four is the one we should be aiming for in a chance meeting. It is the level most likely to produce an enjoyable exchange, which in itself will leave you feeling good. In addition, it's the level most likely to result in follow-up contact and mutual benefit to both people. In other words, it's the level that just might take you another step towards achieving your goal.

To take an active interest in another person, which is what happens at level four, takes a certain generosity of spirit and energy that doesn't always come easily, especially when you're tired or have a lot on your mind. But it's worth making the effort because at the most unlikely moment you could meet the person who holds the key to the success of your venture.

## BE AWARE

Being aware is simply being awake and alert to what is going on around you. It means that, having bumped into someone in a chance meeting, you'll behave in a way that's appropriate and considerate.

Here are some guidelines for polishing up your level of awareness in chance-meeting situations.

## 1. Be Sensitive

It's so easy to get off on the wrong foot and blow any chance of building rapport by saying or doing the wrong thing. Being loud, brash, rude or thoughtless won't get you far. Neither will cracking insensitive jokes or being aloof, patronising or arrogant.

We've all come across people who leave you thinking, Thank goodness I don't have to see him/her again, I couldn't wait to get away. Don't be one of them.

A client told me about a time he was in a restaurant with his family. In the middle of dinner someone recognised him and came over to chat. He became increasingly annoyed as his food got cold, his wife was ignored and his kids were bored while the other man talked on. Needless to say, my client never wanted to see him again.

Trust your better judgement. Before doing or saying anything, just make sure that the situation is right. Wait a minute, observe and always behave with consideration and good manners.

## 2. Don't Be Pushy

If the person you meet by chance is someone you could do business with, don't launch straight into the business angle. Be subtle and keep it social, saving business for later. Being pushy is the fastest way to send the other person running.

I have a client who refuses to attend cocktail parties because he gets inundated with people trying to bend his ear on projects or to sell him their ideas. He's more likely to do business with the person who has a really enjoyable conversation with him about a shared passion or interest.

If you make your primary intention to build rapport and learn then you're far more likely to have a positive outcome, As you build rapport you'll get to the point where it's appropriate to get to questions about work or the opportunity to sell your idea.

Don't feel because you didn't talk much about you or your idea that you somehow blew it. I first met one of my biggest clients when I helped him chase the contents of his briefcase down a windy Chicago street. When we'd gathered up all his papers we went for a coffee and talked about the weather, our families and the cinema for an hour. Work didn't come into it.

### 3. Keep Introductions Brief

When you introduce yourself keep it short and sweet. In her book *How to Work a Room* Susan Roane has some great advice for doing this well. She says that a self-introduction has three purposes:

- To tell people who you are
- To give them a pleasant experience of you
- To engage

She recommends that introductions can be laced with humour and information that will stimulate conversation. She suggests they should be no more than seven to nine seconds long. Include your name and a brief description that tells people who you are and helps them remember you easily. Use a different self-description for different occasions and make what you do sound relevant and interesting to the listener.

For example, John is the Global Head of Risk at a major bank.

To a peer at a financial-markets conference he introduces himself with: 'I'm John Jones – Head of Risk at X Bank'

At a cocktail party for his board members and shareholders he says: 'I'm John Jones, your Global Head of Risk.'

At his daughter's birthday party he sticks to: 'I'm John, Susan's dad'

On the right occasion he adds humour. He introduced himself to a group of fund managers whose funds he is always policing for accuracy and risk control with: 'I'm John, your friendly neighbourhood Rottweiler.'

## 4. Be Yourself

Don't try to be anything other than the normal, natural you. If you suddenly realise that the person you've met by chance could be very important to you, try not to alter the relaxed style you were using when you thought they were no one special. One of the great things about chance meetings is that everyone's equal. The woman who runs a global empire at work is just another mum in the playground.

We start out anonymous at chance meetings and this is what created the special opportunity to build rapport, based on humour, shared interests or the situation you're both in. Don't blow it by becoming awkward, uncomfortable, false or too eager to please once you realise who the person is.

## CREATING A POSITIVE IMPRESSION

Use these seven tips to get any chance meeting off to a great start:

## 1. Make eye contact

Show an interest in someone by making an appropriate level of eye contact when you introduce yourself. Don't overdo it and make the other person uncomfortable; don't avoid eye contact and appear shifty, shy or uninterested.

## 2. Smile

A natural smile is a pretty universal human symbol for 'things are OK, we can talk'.

## 3. Check Your Body

If you've had a bad day and have an attitude to match, make a physical change. Chances are you're hunched, tense and your breathing is shallow. Alter your posture, stand up, move or breathe deeply and you'll be surprised at how much better you feel and how much more easily you engage in conversation.

## 4. Keep Handshaking Light

We all have stories about painful vice-like handshakes or clammy jellyfish ones. Try to keep your touch light but firm and make sure your hands are warm and dry. My hands are often cold for no apparent reason, so I make sure I've warmed them up by keeping contact with something warm, such as my suit or the furniture or a warm cup of tea. Rubbing them gently together before entering a room can help, too. If your hands are a little cold and clammy, make up for it by getting the firmness right.

## 5. Keep it Simple

Start the conversation by commenting on something that is happening around you – the weather, the late train, the new swing in the park – rather than trying to be clever or obscure. That way the other person will find it much easier to respond.

### 6. Do something nice

Perform a random act of kindness – it's a great ice-breaker. Offer part of your newspaper or to get a cup of coffee or tea if you're going anyway. Everyday things, nothing over the top.

### 7. Be patient

Relax into the conversation and don't panic about getting what you want. Enjoy the moment and trust that if something good is meant to come of this then it will happen.

## CREATING THE WRONG IMPRESSION

Here's the behaviour to avoid in a chance meeting:

### 1. Interrogation

Don't just ask question after question, contributing nothing about yourself. This is not a conversation and will quickly put the other person off.

### 2. Homing in on work

Avoid asking,'So, what do you do?' in the first few minutes. Most people don't like to be confronted with this early on. The conversation will come round to it eventually.

### 3. Using obscenities

Even if they use them. This is not the time to match. Keep your end clean and well-mannered.

### 4. Telling Off-Colour Jokes

Unless you're absolutely sure you won't offend, avoid jokes that involve sex, race, religion and politics, because the truth is, you can never be sure.

### 5. Having Bad Breath
If you've been drinking alcohol, remember that you probably smell offensive to someone who hasn't been drinking. Keep your distance and, if necessary, acknowledge it. Same with the garlic you had for lunch.

### 6. Gossiping
Gossip can be entertaining, but it can also leave others feeling uncomfortable. And no one trusts a gossip. Don't lower yourself to that level.

### 7. Selling
The early stage of a chance meeting is not the time to try to sell a product, idea or message.

## FOLLOWING UP

Only you know if it is the right thing to follow up a chance meeting. If you've exchanged numbers, cards or invitations then obviously it's fine. If not then you have to gauge whether the exchange was friendly enough for a follow-up call to be acceptable. If you didn't speak of meeting again then my advice is not to wait too long. A phone call within forty-eight hours is more likely to get a meeting than a letter a week later. It's easy for the other person to forget about meeting you in the flotsam of everyday life.

I have a friend who had a wonderful chance meeting that she followed up by sending a gift of a little stuffed animal in the post. Apparently they had discussed stuffed animals and my friend liked the idea of being a bit creative. Unfortunately the person who received it couldn't remember my friend or the relevance of this and didn't respond. When they met a year later at a conference it all made sense. The moral of the story is to keep it simple and follow up quickly.

## SEIZE THE CHANCE

Chance meetings are all around us. New and interesting people and great opportunities are dished up to us daily if we're willing to spot them and seize them.

Don't be someone who sits on the sidelines and says, 'I never seem to meet anyone interesting.' If that's you then it's time to try a little harder. The opportunities are there; you're just not tuning in to them.

Take off your blinkers and look around. Whatever you're doing, there are usually other people around doing it too and a thousand potentially enjoyable and useful chance meetings waiting to be had.

Whatever it is you want to succeed in, achieve or communicate to the world, chance meetings can be a valuable tool to help get you there.

# PART THREE

# MAKE-OR-BREAK MOMENTS

# 12

# PLANNING FOR YOUR MAKE-OR-BREAK MOMENT

*It's not the will to win that's important. It's the will to prepare to win that really separates those who wish and dream from those who make it happen*

**US FOOTBALL COACH DICK TOMEY**

For most people who are pursuing a dream, a goal or an idea they want to bring to fruition, there is a make-or-break moment. This is the moment when the person you most need to see, the one who can help make your goal a reality, agrees to meet you and listen to what you have to say. Perhaps you get the chance to address the audience you want to reach, you get the interview for that longed-for job, a potential sponsor for your charity agrees to see you or an agent agrees to look at your book. Whatever form your make-or-break moment takes, you know that succeeding at this point will make a huge difference to you and your idea. In an ideal world – and this is possible more often than you think – you have the 'deal' done before you get to your make-or-break moment. You've done so much homework and made such an effort to build rapport with the right people that the make-or-break moment itself becomes a formality.

Of course, this make-or-break moment is only one of a series of milestones and events that are part of your journey to success.

As you move towards achieving what you set out to do there will almost certainly be other make-or-break moments along the way. Each one will fill you with a mixture of excitement, anxiety, delight, dread and most emotions in between! Not all of them will work out perfectly, some may simply be a useful learning experience. But it's that first make-or-break moment that can have the greatest impact. That's why you need to plan for it very carefully. The last thing you want is to reach a crucial moment badly prepared and blow it.

To help you be as ready as you can be I've put together a seven-step action plan. You've made it this far, now use the action plan to get the results you want from this make-or-break moment – and the other important milestones ahead. Most people don't know how to plan properly. They skirt round the edges or miss out vital stages. But if you find 20 per cent more time to plan then you'll make an 80 per cent difference to the way things turn out.

## YOUR SEVEN-STEP ACTION PLAN

Follow these steps in the order they appear because that's how they'll work best.

### Step One: Make Sure this is the Right Person to See

One of the most common mistakes is to organise a meeting with the wrong person or people. By wrong people I mean those who aren't in a position to make decisions or who would not directly benefit from the presentation or idea.

Lots of people set up a meeting with whoever they can get hold of in an organisation, rather than the person they really need to see. They arrange to talk to someone lower down the hierarchy in the hope that they will have some influence or help them get access to the person who counts. Occasionally this works, but mostly it doesn't and a lot of time is wasted. Many people do this because they believe the right person is too busy or important to see them. I've seen this happen at a very senior level, but believe me it's nonsense.

I have a friend who had been trying for months to get his business going – a firm specialising in adventure travel for company executives. He had a great idea, a solid business plan and plenty of potential clients. Yet he was struggling to get any companies to sign up for his trips.

After talking with him for a while, I realised that he was arranging meetings with the wrong people in the organisations. He was seeing people he could get meetings with and hoping he could talk his way around or get introduced to the right people once he 'got in'. But it wasn't working. The people he needed to meet were the ones who would directly benefit and who had the money to pay for it out of their budgets. He was shy about approaching these people and fooling himself into thinking that activity alone would somehow get him where he wanted to go.

Once he saw what he was doing wrong he found the courage to approach the people he really needed to see – with great success. In the end it was a simple matter of picking up the phone and asking for someone else in the organisation. The right person.

Take a few minutes to ask yourself the following questions:

- Is this a person who can benefit from what I have to offer?
- Is this person in a position to make the decision I need?
- Is this person someone with influence, and how might they use it?

It's important to sit and think about the sort of people who would benefit from your idea or message. For example, a friend of mine who has her own interior-design business knows that the people she wants to work with and who are most likely to benefit from her particular services

- Live within a twenty-mile radius of her office
- Are able and willing to pay her fees
- Are in the market for projects of a value more than x
- Want a Victorian feel to their interior design
- May have other potential contacts she can meet

Lots of time and effort is wasted on the wrong meetings. Make sure yours has the right potential.

## Step Two: Get the Ball Rolling

You can affect the way the person or people you're going to meet will view you by doing a few clever things in advance. Choose the right ways to get the ball rolling and they'll have a positive impression of you before the meeting begins. It will also help them to keep you in mind, as the meeting may be arranged weeks in advance.

Here are some things I've done and have seen others do:

- If you have to send anything beforehand – a presentation or outline – be sure it can 'stand alone'. In other words, that it's clear, straightforward and self-explanatory, so that anyone can look at it and get a good idea of what the meeting will be about
- Send a letter reminding them of when you will be there as well as some useful information about you

- Send a clue that gives a flavour of what you want to talk about,
  such as a newspaper clipping, video, website address or leaflet

## Step Three: Do Your Homework

A colleague of mine used to say, 'Never pitch to strangers.'
This means you should make an effort to get to know as
much as you can in advance about the person or people
you're meeting.

This is the most important step of all because the more
you know about them the more likely you are to meet their
needs and succeed.

Here is a checklist of questions you should try to answer.
You won't be able to get answers to all of them but use them
as a guide to find out as much as you can:

- Who will be at the meeting?
- What are they like?
- How powerful are they? For instance, can they give you a
  decision?
- What's the company/organisation like? What are its values,
  culture, history, etc.?
- If foreign, are there cultural differences you should take on
  board, things you shouldn't say or do?
- How much do they know about you/your idea?
- Why are they interested in it?
- What will they get out of it?
- What do they want or need?
- How much money can they spend/give?
- What else might influence their decision?

If possible, get hold of a photo of the person you're meeting.
It can be very comforting to know in advance what they look
like.

I can't stress how important it is that you spend time
getting to know the people you'll be meeting, before you

meet them. Imagine how good it feels to enter a room knowing that what you're going to talk about will interest the people there and knowing what the potential obstacles might be.

One of the best ways to gather a little information in advance is to ask the person who invited you to the meeting. This may be someone who will be there or an assistant. Chances are they won't mind you calling to ask a few carefully thought-out questions. If the call is successful, you will have gleaned useful information and still be able to call back if you need to. So many people don't bother to do this; they're so happy to have arranged the meeting that it doesn't occur to them to find out more information before they go to it. But these extra phone calls can make a huge difference to the outcome.

## Step Four: Know Your Objective

Before you go to your make-or-break meeting it's important to know exactly what you want from it as well as what it's possible to achieve. This may sound obvious but you'd be surprised how many people don't!

Of course they know the overall goal they want to achieve. For instance:

- I want my script filmed
- I want to climb Everest
- I want to get the contract to design the Japanese Gardens
- I want funding for my nursery school

But on the way to the big goal there are always steps and smaller goals to achieve. Success is usually the culmination of a series of events, and your make-or-break moment, important though it is, is only one of them.

That's why you need to be clear about what you'd like from this specific meeting. For instance:

- I want the commissioning editor to agree to talk to the head of drama at the TV station about my script
- I want the potential sponsor to agree to talk to his board about putting some money into my expedition
- I want the estate manager to agree to show the stately-home owner my Japanese garden designs
- I want the finance director to agree to recommend that my nursery be given support

Once you know exactly what you want to accomplish, based on who will be there and the powers they have, you can decide what to say to have the maximum impact. Your goal should be practical, sensible and attainable. Try writing it out in one strong, positive sentence.

Persuasion usually boils down to a series of agreements, so decide what you need agreed in this meeting and concentrate on that.

### Step Five: Collect the Right Information

It's time to identify and organise the information that will be most convincing and persuasive to the people you want to influence.

Because you've done your homework you are more likely to understand how much and what kind of information would be most appropriate and cut out anything unnecessary.

Ask yourself if you really need to spend time on certain things or exploring certain areas. A manufacturer I was working with recently told me about a meeting he'd organised with a client. He had a new idea to pitch to this client and had decided to give him three options. Each option would be carefully explained by a different expert and the client would be given three written outlines.

I pointed out that this was a lot to pack into an hour-long

meeting and would leave the client with over a hundred pages to read. The manufacturer knew his client well, they had worked together for years and the client trusted him. I suggested that he need recommend only *one* option – the best one – to the client. This would mean only one expert and one brief written summary. Shorter, sharper, to the point and everyone is happy.

The message is never give more information than is necessary to make your point and achieve your objective.

## Step Six: Structure Your Message

It's time to choose a structure for your message, based on the time available. Will you be making a recommendation or just informing? Should you be direct about what you want or build up to it with some background information?

So often I see people back out of an opportunity to tell others exactly what they want, thinking that with enough 'information' the other people will somehow know. Trouble is, they often don't and the person walks away disappointed. So, have the courage to make a recommendation or request, if it's appropriate. Be brave and tell people what you want. But remember that if you're going to make a recommendation or request, keep it simple and clear; don't make it too long and complicated.

Structure gives you flexibility and control; that's why it's good to make a plan. Of course, you don't have to stick to it rigidly; it will simply give you a basis to work from and something to help you get back on track when you feel nervous or lose the thread.

Keep in mind that people listen better when you have

- Prepared them to receive your message
- Delivered what you said you would
- Made sure they have received and understood it

These principles are fundamental in every situation in which you want to communicate with someone else. If something is misunderstood or goes wrong then the chances are you've slipped up in one of these areas.

Don't be shy about having the structure of your message or presentation in front of you on a piece of paper as you speak. Write your key points in boxes rather than word for word.

Notes are always acceptable. Think them as the map of your message. Go back to chapter 9 if you want to remind yourself of the kinds of structures you might use.

This is also the time to include any visual aids you might want as part of your message or presentation. Would it be useful to use a video, a flip-chart or a computer-generated presentation?

When deciding whether to use visual aids, make sure you don't put them in just to fill time or to make your presentation feel bigger. Visual aids should always be an addition to the substance of the message, an extra that is helpful but not vital. Think about whether any visual aids you have really add to the message. Make sure they don't take the focus off you, because you are the most important thing. The person or people you're meeting need to see and hear from you without too many distractions.

### Step Seven: Are You Ready?

Now is the time to check your whole message for consistency, clarity and simplicity.

Sit down alone or with a friend, go through what you are going to say, present or deliver and see if you believe it. Check it for mistakes and then ask yourself the hard questions you could possibly face. Is there anything deep and dark someone could ask you that you need to be prepared for? What's the worst question someone could ask you?

Prepare more than one way to answer each question and be ready for the embarrassing comments or questions you hope won't happen!

Make sure also that you're ready to talk about fees and costs. This area often leaves people stuttering, unprepared or embarrassed, and finding themselves agreeing to charge less than they're worth. There's more on how to decide what you charge in the next chapter.

If there is any more preparation you need to do then do it now. Make that call, do that extra piece of research, be sure that you've done all the homework you need to do in order to produce a really sound message.

## REHEARSE

Now that you've prepared your message it's time to rehearse it. You need to be prepared to run through the whole thing at least three times.

Rehearsing is not just for stand-up presentations or formal public speaking. It is valuable any time you have to deliver a message to anyone, face to face or on the phone.

Why? Because when you rehearse you will find things that need adjusting, emphasising and de-emphasising. It starts to become real for you and is the beginning of making it real for your listeners.

Even if what you will be presenting is a simple message, request or plan, it still helps to rehearse it. Anything important we need to communicate to someone else deserves to be rehearsed so that we can give it our best shot.

That's why I want you to take rehearsing seriously. In my experience, it can be the difference between you succeeding or failing in your make-or-break moment.

## Here are some fundamental principles to remember about rehearsing:

- Rehearsing will free you to perform at your best. If you've rehearsed thoroughly you'll be able to take the focus off yourself and to listen to and learn from others
- If things do go wrong – and they always do at some point – then they won't go as badly wrong if you've rehearsed. Without rehearsing, a wrong move can send you totally off track
- Remember that all the best performers, whether they're actors, athletes, politicians or public speakers, rehearse in order to perform at their best
- If you haven't rehearsed, it will show. You'll be more disorganised, inauthentic or mechanical. To refuse to rehearse shows a touch of arrogance, which won't impress anyone
- Rehearsing puts memory in your muscles. Things are always easier if you've done them before. Give your body a chance to help you succeed

## Plenty of people refuse to rehearse. Here are the top five excuses they use:

- I work better under pressure
- I don't have time
- If I rehearse, my style becomes artificial
- I like to do it in my head
- I can't do it if I have to pretend

And here are the most common reasons clients give for turning people down:

- They just didn't seem to work well together as a team
- I couldn't understand what was important to her and what it meant to me
- He/she didn't seem to know a lot about our needs
- She/he seemed really nervous and disorganised

- He/she couldn't answer our questions or objections to our satisfaction

All these reasons are related to preparation and rehearsal. Don't let this happen to you.

## So, how do you rehearse?

Here's my guide to getting your rehearsals right:

- Plan your rehearsal time well ahead of your meeting
- Ask a friend to come and listen while you do it
- If possible, create an environment similar to the one you will be in. For instance, sit round a large table, use a similar-sized room or line up a few chairs in front of you. If you're going to be in a public venue, go and see it and spend a little time there
- Don't just rehearse what you have written or prepared. Rehearse answering questions, too. Remember to include the obvious ones as well as the most difficult ones you might encounter
- Use rehearsal time to look for areas to improve, but look for your strengths, too. It will encourage you to know that there are some things you're doing really well
- Ask the friend who has been your audience to give you feedback on the good and bad points and the overall feel

Don't think of rehearsing as a chore. It can be great fun and is an investment in getting what you want and making things happen in the right way.

Finally, don't skip any angles when you rehearse. I've done this – to my cost. I was once due to give a presentation to a group of 500 sales representatives at a conference, most of them men. I rehearsed well in the auditorium and felt prepared. But I did one unrehearsed thing that changed the whole presentation from good to awful in two seconds. I decided at the last minute that instead of presenting from behind the podium as everyone else had, I would present sitting on a stool next to the podium. I thought this would allow me to move around the stage and would create a different tone for my presentation.

Boy, did I change the tone. What I didn't realise was that when I sat on the stool, my dress went up so high that it was an enormous distraction. I did my whole presentation looking as if I was doing an advert for stockings.

I only realised what I'd done afterwards when someone eventually told me. I had really upset the chairman and his wife who were sitting in the front row and who thought I was doing this on purpose to use my 'feminine wiles'. I was horrified and very, very embarrassed. So, make sure you check every single aspect, even the way you're going to sit, well ahead of time.

OK. You've planned. You've rehearsed. You're as ready as you can be. It's time to go for it!

# 13

# GO FOR IT!

*Life is like playing a violin in public and learning the instrument as one goes on*
**SAMUEL BUTLER**

You've arrived! Your make-or-break moment is here and success – we hope – is just around the corner. You've done your homework, prepared what you want to say or present and, hopefully, rehearsed until you're totally at home with your material.

In this chapter I'll give you some last-minute tips that will help you arrive at your make-or-break moment in great form and ready for anything. Then we'll take a look at what actually happens during your make-or-break meeting, what you want out of it and how to ensure you get it.

Finally, we'll take a look at what happens afterwards and the most useful way to review what happened.

## LAST-MINUTE TIPS

Here's a checklist to help you feel at your best when you face your make-or-break moment:

- Make sure you get a good night's sleep the night before
- Don't drink alcohol the night before
- Eat a healthy, light meal beforehand, so that you're not hungry or over-full
- Think positively: expect things to go well and believe in yourself. Remind yourself of past successes
- Accept your nervousness as natural and normal. You'll never get rid of all nervousness, so see it as your ally
- Dress comfortably and wear clothes you feel good in
- Don't rehearse on the day, simply remind yourself of the key points
- Breathe deeply – it will clear your head
- Make sure fun is part of your plan – enjoy it!

That's it. You're ready. Behave with confidence and always be your own authentic self.

## Finally

- Remember that people want you to succeed
- Remember that what you have to offer will benefit the people you are talking to
- Remember that you deserve success

## ACHIEVING RESULTS

What do you want to achieve from your make-or-break moment? The chances are that it involves some kind of agreement. An agreement doesn't necessarily involve tangible results, but at the very least it involves a mutual understanding of what will happen next.

Most agreements also involve money. Perhaps you want your services or business to be used and this will involve charging fees. Perhaps you want sponsorship, backing or support. Perhaps you're going for the job of your dreams, asking someone to exhibit your paintings, persuading someone to buy what you create or sell, or hoping for a contract. All of these will involve money at some stage. That's why it's vital that you know two things. First, how to reach an agreement. And second, how to talk about money. Whatever your goal, dream or message, making it happen is going to involve reaching agreements along the line. And some or all of those agreements are almost certainly going to involve money.

All too often, people leave make-or-break meetings and realise they haven't actually got a clear agreement about what happens next. Perhaps they've been told, 'We'll be in touch.' But what does this mean? When will they hear something?

The lack of clear agreement is especially true when money is involved. The subject may not have been raised at all, or it might have been tagged hastily on to the end of the meeting. And you may have accepted a lower fee than you're worth or want to charge, just because you feel the whole subject is difficult and embarrassing.

A talented potter I know was so bowled over when a chain store ordered some of his designs that he undercharged by a big margin. The offer took him by surprise, he simply hadn't expected such a good result. At the time he felt he would have gladly given the designs away for the pleasure of seeing them in high-street stores. But when he'd had a moment to calm down, he began to regret undervaluing his work.

Don't let this happen to you! If you're confident and at ease talking about money you're likely to come away with a better agreement, one you feel good about.

## REACHING AGREEMENT

Before we look specifically at money agreements, let's be clear what an agreement is.

Most people are uncomfortable with the tension they feel when it comes to the crunch, so they back away from it, skirt round it or rush it.

However, some people are really good at it. You can choose to be one of them as long as you understand what is going on and remain calm and objective. Keep this important fact in mind: gaining agreement doesn't 'happen' at the end of the meeting in some big orchestrated finale. Trying to do this is what puts so much pressure on people and creates so much tension. Effective agreement starts happening from the beginning of the meeting and is affected by everything you do and say. Gaining agreement is dependent on creating rapport and is a series of events and mini-agreements that happen along the way. To gain agreement you plan for it and you listen for clues and act on them. If you let it sneak up on you or try to shove it in as an afterthought it's likely to go wrong.

Gaining agreement is about neatly closing the communication loop. So often we think we've completed our meeting or presentation or conversation, but if we look closely there's been no real agreement about what happens next. We can be left thinking, What did we agree?

Most of the people I speak to who work for big companies say that many of their meetings are a waste of time because no real or productive agreement is reached. Often the decision is simply to refer the issue or to have another meeting. There are plenty of well-paid people who sit in meeting rooms wondering why they're there, or who leave meetings wondering what they're supposed to do next, or thinking something has been agreed only to find that it hasn't.

The good news is that there are some things you can do

to make gaining agreement and closing the communication loop easier:

- To reach a meaningful, fair and lasting agreement it is important to know as much as you can about the values of the people you're dealing with. This knowledge will help you plan what to say and choose your direction during any discussion or agreement
- Go into a meeting, presentation or conversation with a clear idea about what a successful outcome looks like. Be able to articulate it clearly
- Remind yourself at various points of the meeting about the agreement you hope for by the end
- At the end, check that the outcome has actually happened
- Stand back and detach emotionally from what is going on. Most of the tension associated with gaining agreement happens because the people involved take things too personally

Things that can get in the way of reaching clear agreement include:

- Lack of preparation
- Getting distracted or caught up on a trivial issue
- Missing a valuable piece of information or insight through failing to ask enough questions
- Giving away too much, not valuing the services/talent on offer
- Losing control of the meeting

If you've done your homework and prepared well you're far more likely to reach the agreement you want. Make sure you know what it is and make sure the meeting is always heading in the direction of this agreement and isn't thrown off track. Have the agreement you want at the back of your mind throughout; don't let it be something you remember at the last minute.

Build up to the agreement with questions such as

- What would you like me to do?
- How would you like us to do it?
- Are you prepared to agree to this?
- Can we reach an agreement?
- Are you happy to go ahead with this?

At the end of the meeting make sure that everyone understands what has been agreed. Don't leave anything fuzzy or vague. Use phrases such as

- So, are we all agreed that. . .
- I understand we're agreeing to . . .
- I can expect to hear from you on x date with a decision
- You'd like me to send the follow-up tomorrow and we'll meet again on x day
- I'm delighted. Can we put that agreement in writing?

Whenever possible, follow up the meeting by writing to confirm what has been agreed. You can do this in the form of a thank-you, such as: 'Thank you for seeing me. I'm delighted that you've agreed to . . .'

A meeting, conversation or phone call that ends with a clear agreement is a success, even if that agreement is only a small step along your path.

## Reaching Agreement about Money

Agreements about money give us the most trouble and are where we need to be most brave. So, let's look at those in more detail.

Money is a sensitive issue because it's so closely linked to our own personal values and beliefs. To charge others for your work you've got to believe that you're worth it and that your work is good. Even if, rather than charging, you're looking for funding for a project or for a charitable donation, you still need a good helping of self-belief, as well as a strong belief in your project or cause.

If you're charging for your work then the first step is to decide on your fees before the meeting. To do this you need to

- Start by adding up your production costs. These might include travel, materials, heating and lighting, etc.
- Next, look at what others are charging for a similar service. If you're just starting out, choose the mid-range of these fees to place your own fee
- Think about your personal financial goals and plans. These will affect what you charge. For instance, do you have a minimum amount you need to earn? Are you willing to charge less for a job you'll enjoy?
- What information do you have about the client's financial position and values? Are they on a set budget? Will they be able to afford what you charge?
- If you don't trust yourself to charge fairly, ask for the advice of a financially astute friend or colleague

If you're looking for funding for a project, you'll still need to provide as much information as possible, including any production costs and fees involved.

Now let's focus on some guidelines to keep in mind when you find yourself faced with gaining agreement about money.

### Be prepared to have the discussion

The one thing I find my clients are least prepared for in their meetings is the discussion about money. It's almost as if they think it will take place at another time or won't happen at all. But why would you want to get almost all the way up the mountain and not have brought enough crampons to get to the top?

Be ready for the discussion about money and welcome it as a signal that things are going well. Be prepared to bring the subject up yourself if the other person doesn't.

Before you go into the meeting or presentation, decide on some parameters. First, come up with what your best possible outcome could be. This is what you would get if everything went your way. Then think of your absolute worst possible outcome – what would it take for you to walk away? Now work towards the middle. Prioritise the aspects of the discussion that are important to you and what aspects are important to the people you will be agreeing with. Most people only know about what is important to them, but that's only half the deal.

One of the worst things you can do is mumble-stumble through the discussion about money or appear to lack confidence when asking for it.

Years ago, when I was first starting out, I made that classic mistake of answering the question about fees with 'Usually we charge . . .' and proceeded to explain my way out of any form of fair agreement. Ouch.

Be aware of it if you're mumbling, fidgeting or behaving in a nervous way and stop.

Have ready what you want to say. Keep it brief and clear. Say it and then pause, while maintaining eye contact. One of the biggest mistakes people make is to have their answer ready and then keep rambling on after they've said it.

### Understand that people value different things

Don't assume that because you think something is valuable, someone else feels the same way. You need to 'qualify' – which means to be sure about the other person's expectations.

Imagine that you're selling your house. You see your prize rose garden as a particularly valuable and attractive feature, but the potential buyers want to pave it over to put in a pool. To them the rose garden means nothing. Each side in this negotiation has a different idea of what is valuable.

Or, to give another example, the detailed report you spent a lot of time preparing and feel very proud of might mean nothing to the decision-maker who wants a one-page summary.

This is why you need to find out which aspects of what you do or offer have a value to the other person. To do this you need to find out about them in advance, to listen carefully to what they say and to ask questions during the meeting.

I call this the 'Jill factor'. My friend Jill is incredibly adept at gaining clear agreement with her clients and colleagues. She manages to stay cool, clear and objective even in the most heated discussions. How? She prepares well and she listens for clues. Most people don't. She makes sure she understands how and what the other person values. Then she can begin to decide what she can give, and, most importantly, what she can gain.

Jill also told me about something called 'value-based pricing'. This means that you should consider what your services are actually worth to the client. How might they benefit financially from your services? How can you charge on this basis?

When helping clients to win a contract, I have often charged another type of price – a fixed fee rather than an hourly rate. This is a lump sum based on the value of the work they're trying to win and is only charged if we are successful. In this way, my charge is based on the value of the work to the client.

An Australian businessman who ran a successful graphic-design business designed a label for a can of soup for a major food manufacturer. The food manufacturer came back to him and said they had never paid so much for a design and questioned his fee. He told them that he would gladly accept half a cent per item sold as an alternative. When the food manufacturer went back and did the sums they realised they would end up paying the designer millions. They decided to pay his fee, which suddenly seemed much better value. But be warned: in order to benefit fully from value-based pricing, you need to understand your value to the buyer and to be bold and brave. Otherwise don't try it!

When you're discussing money and someone says, 'That seems really expensive,' don't panic. Think about what might be influencing that comment. Ask questions. Jill's advice is that, rather than reduce the price, be more explicit. If you say, 'My fee includes x and y. What would you like me to leave out?' then the client can choose. They may well decide to pay the full fee once they see what it covers.

We are often much too quick to reduce our prices. One of my colleagues told me about an experience he had with a major professional-services firm. The client mentioned that he had a problem with the price. My colleague was quick to jump in and offer to 'see what he could do' to reduce the price. The client interrupted and said, 'You aren't listening. I don't think you are charging enough.' So, ask before reacting!

### Keep talking until everyone is happy

There is another aspect of gaining agreement. You may recall from chapter 8 on sticky situations that sometimes we can think we're talking about the same thing when we're not. When this is happening, conversations can go on and on, or you can have several meetings and never seem to reach agreement.

If you don't know what people's concerns are, you

will never be able to address them fully. You have to listen carefully for clues to see if you understand each other and are talking about the same things.

If you find yourself in a meeting where things are a little 'flabby' and the conversation is not reaching closure, take back some control and focus the other person by asking, What are you thinking now?' This may give the person a chance to tell you something new or important and may provide a new angle that allows you to move towards agreement.

There is an old negotiation adage: 'Nothing is agreed until everything is agreed.' To reach complete and happy agreement listen clearly to what the other person really wants. Be sure you have addressed all the issues – yours and theirs.

### Expect that people will try to manage your expectations

Because reaching agreement can be such a loaded subject you have to expect that there may be some tactics involved. By tactics, I mean things people may do to affect what you expect from the agreement. There are all kinds of games people play in order to lower your expectations.

Here are some common examples:

- Deferring decision-making to an invisible third party
- Audibly gasping or looking angry and shaking their head when they hear your price
- Scowling and immediately telling you there are other people competing for this business
- Telling you they will have to pay in instalments over a period of time
- Suggesting you have overestimated the work involved

And there are hundreds of other tactics. The important thing is to see them for what they are. Test them. Never rush to lower your price. Be aware of things you might fall for too easily. Instead, remain calm and wait before you respond. Check, ask and be sure it's not just a tactic.

## REVIEW

When you've finished your meeting or presentation, it is time to review the whole thing. This is when you ask yourself what went well or badly and what you can do better next time. Sometimes it's tempting to put that experience in a drawer and not think about it again, especially if you feel it hasn't gone well. But by taking what you learn from this experience with you to the next, you develop your experience and skills. So, take a little time to review before you move on.

Here's how to do a brief and effective review of your meeting.

First ask yourself the following questions:

- Did you meet the right people?
- Did you understand your listeners?
- Was your objective clear?
- Did you have the right evidence and information to support your idea and recommendations?
- Did you choose the right structure?
- Did your visual aids do what you wanted them to?
- Could you have prepared better in any way?
- Did anything come out of your meeting or presentation that you weren't expecting? How did you deal with it?
- Did you reach agreement?
- Did you achieve your objective?
- Have you followed up?

Congratulate yourself on all the aspects that went well. If you are unhappy with any of your answers, work out why and look at what you might have done differently. Make a note of anything that will be useful for your next make-or-break moment. Discuss it with someone. Tell them what you would do differently.

The next part of your review is to answer and follow up any questions or requests that may have come out of the meeting. Do it right away. Doing it quickly shows interest and a positive attitude. Make sure you understand what you are following up on – even if you need to contact the person directly to double-check.

If you're waiting to hear from the other person, find reasons to be back in touch. Write immediately, thanking them for their time and trouble and saying you are looking forward to future contact or to hearing their decision.

There is a rule of thumb that I've applied many times and that is, if there is no contact from them within two weeks, something has gone amiss. I've seen clients feel a sense of relief after a big meeting, 'Whew, we've done it,' and then wait passively for an answer. This is asking for trouble. Keep the energy up, and keep your intention strong by finding creative and meaningful ways to keep yourself at the forefront of things. If you do this they're far more likely to make a decision or get back to you. Often decisions are made after the meeting – a colleague once said that 'The pitch starts after the meeting.' Don't stop. See the end as a new beginning.


## IN CONCLUSION. . .

When you reach your make-or-break moment remember that gaining agreement is one of your greatest challenges. Whatever the situation – meeting, phone call, conversation – what matters is to achieve a result. Keep this in mind and stay focussed on what you want to achieve. View the whole interaction as a series of moves towards agreement and then make sure everyone knows what the agreement is.

That way you make-or-break moment won't be wasted and you'll be a step nearer to achieving your goal.

Remember also to be flexible where appropriate. You may not come away with exactly the agreement you set out to achieve, but you might have something worthwhile, interesting and useful.

# 14

# WHAT NEXT?

*Be humble for you are made of dung*
*Be noble for you are made of stars*
**SERBIAN PROVERB**

Communication is the key to achieving our goals. It's what fills the gap between dreaming and doing, between hoping for and achieving, and between thinking about it and making it happen.

Communication, at its best, is the ability to make yourself clear, get others on your side and persuade them to do or give you what you want. I hope this book has been able to help you achieve this. If it's helped to bring you closer to achieving your goal then it has done its job.

The secret of change is to take it on in bite-sized chunks. Do one new thing at a time and make that stick before you go on to another thing and so on, so that each new thing becomes second nature. Don't wait too long between things, push yourself to get into the habit of learning. Keep going, be patient, and pretty soon you won't have to think about these things any more, you'll just do them. They'll become part of the choices you make on a day-to-day basis. Do one new thing and do it well and you'll start to see changes.

You'll continue to refine. This is just a start. Add in a few more new things and you'll find you have the power to make wonderful things happen.

**I cannot stress strongly enough that the single most important thing you can do to improve your communication skills is to take the focus off yourself.**
It takes an effort to do this, because the main emphasis in the world today is on satisfying the self. We are encouraged to go after what we want first and to think of others, if we do so at all, second.

Of course, understanding yourself, your own desires, needs and motivations is important. So is knowing what you want and having the courage to pursue it. But the really big challenge is to understand how what you want benefits others. People will make decisions about whether to involve themselves with you on the basis of their desires, values and motivations. Your efforts and ideas will be ineffectual unless you can understand and respond to this.

Start to understand what makes others tick and what they want, and you will soon find that people begin to respond to you differently and that the things you want will begin to happen.

**The idea of improving your communication skills is to get it right more often**
There is nothing fancy or complicated about this. In fact, that's part of its charm – it's so simple.

To start with you have to strip back the layers of behaviours that you know aren't serving you. Maybe you've been over-coached, over-therapied, over-educated, over-worried, over-worked or even over-confident. If I asked you right now, you would very quickly be able to tell me about two or three things that you do regularly that don't serve you.

Maybe you procrastinate about that next step, take your health for granted, hold grudges or stay in that job you hate.

If you were willing to get rid of these two or three behaviours, you would give yourself the break you need to make some wonderful things happen and really allow your communication to work for you. Why? Because finding the courage to make changes gives you momentum, energy and the determination to move forward.

Don't get me wrong – this isn't about curing the human condition before you can move on. It's more about rethinking what you've packed for the trip. Make the load a bit lighter and bring more of what you really need.

I'm not sure that we can ever expect to get it right as often as we'd like to. But we can make a start and get it right more often.

### You already have what you need in order to achieve whatever you want.

The trick is to take that leap of faith and believe it before you see it. When you begin to trust that you have what you need, that you are complete and ready, then you'll begin to act in a different way. Your confidence, motivation and belief in yourself will increase.

You will become a more successful communicator, improve the quality of your relationships and win more by building genuine rapport with people.

Never hesitate to ask for help from your friends – those you know now and the ones you will discover. Be open and comfortable with the idea of asking for and receiving feedback. Listen to it. It is one of the fastest and least painful ways to cultivate humility.

Above all else, learning to communicate well should be fun. Enjoying what you do, rather than fear, is the best motivation. Be relentless in your desire to align your strengths with the way you spend your time and the people you spend it with. Because if you're having fun, you're more likely to be successful.

I hope you will treat this book as a well-thumbed guide to pick up and dig into whenever your life calls for it. I hope it will give you encouragement and support as you pursue your goals.

Enjoy yourself. Do good work. Communicate well.